Uprising of Goats

Uprising of Goats

DIANE GLANCY

WIPF & STOCK · Eugene, Oregon

UPRISING OF GOATS

Copyright © 2014 Diane Glancy. All rights reserved. Except for brief quotations in critical publications or reviews, no part of this book may be reproduced in any manner without prior written permission from the publisher. Write: Permissions. Wipf and Stock Publishers, 199 W. 8th Ave., Suite 3, Eugene, OR 97401.

Wipf and Stock
An Imprint of Wipf and Stock Publishers
199 W. 8th Ave., Suite 3
Eugene, OR 97401

www.wipfandstock.com

ISBN 13: 978-1-62564-720-7

Manufactured in the U.S.A.   07/23/2014

> ...they're notorious
> for interpreting the Bible to suit themselves.
> —Denise Duhamel, "Noah and Joan"

Contents

A Chapter in Which the Beginning Begins to Shred | 1

Hispera: Noah's Wife, A Chapter Floating on the Water | 4

A Chapter in Which Things Start to Go Bad between Us | 12

Hagar: The Little Goat Trail, A Chapter in Which Land Appears | 14

Ishmael Had a Box Of Crayons | 18

Dorcas: The Closets of Heaven, A Chapter in Which Fabric Is a Weighty Matter | 22

I Dorcas' Life | 24

A Chapter in Which an Afterword to Dorcas and a Divorce Begins | 36

II Dorcas' Death | 38

A Chapter in Which an Afterword to Dorcas Continues | 43

III Peter Calls Dorcas Back | 46

A Chapter in Which an Afterword to Dorcas Continues | 59

IV Dorcas Returns from Death | 61

A Chapter in Which Afterword to Dorcas Ends | 75

Michal: A Stone I Could Not Lift, A Chapter Found on the Slope of a Steep Hill | 78

A Chapter in Which There Is an Afterword to Michal | 88

Anna: A Chapter in Which a Raisin Cake Is Wrapped in Cloth | 90

Afterword to Anna, A Chapter in Which Tenure Was Received | 95

A Chapter in Which a Group of Women See Christ's Death | 97

A Chapter in Which a Sabbatical and a Divorce Appear | 98

The Parting, A Chapter in Which the Four Daughters of Philip Are Called by Name | 101

Philipa | 102

Clauda | 112

A Chapter in Which There Is Fellowship | 121

Prudah | 123

Lucina | 134

A Chapter in Which There Is an Afterword to the Daughters of Philip | 140

Miriam: Seven Days in Leprosy Camp, A Chapter Stuck in the Desert | 149

A Chapter in Which There Is an Afterword to Miriam | 161

Uprising, A Chapter in Which the End Is Reached | 164

Acknowledgments | 167

A Chapter in Which the Beginning Begins to Shred

The ocean came over my bed at night.

I would say, first of all, the voices were in it. They floated among the fish.

Later, the voices also came to me in travel. Then they were picked up in ordinary places of anyday. I never knew when they were coming, or who the words belonged to when they first arrived. It was apparent that there were several voices speaking, and soon I found that the pieces began to fit together. Sooner, it seemed, I found the voices became a net. I was cast into it. "I will make you a fisher of men" (Matt 4:19). But I was the catch they caught.

I had no one to talk to. By then, I was separated from my husband. My daughters were in their last year of school before college. Often, they were out with friends. I had no one in the house but the voices. Otherwise I would not have heard them. I was in the religious studies department at a college with a Christian foundation. There was a pull away from the voices, and a pull back.

Often I looked into the heavens with my bare eyes. It was a bowling alley without straight lanes. God and the angels and Jesus were there, and the Holy Spirit like a wind off the coast, stirring up fog or a desert sandstorm. God's thoughts are his thoughts. My thoughts are mine. If only they weren't so far apart. I thought to ignore him. To not consider. To be my own.

Who were these upstart voices? Already I wanted to roll them away with jelly beans or jujubes or jolly ranchers. They were trouble already. They would be easy to defeat. It was darkness that called them to it. It was darkness I could follow. They were not upstarts, they said. No. No. I saw they were not.

It was darkness I was made for. Darkness that I sought. To go in darkness took only headlights. There was an island in the sea to pull into when I was tired of driving. I saw the fir trees with their arms out. Their hands grasping for air. Who taught them prayer? Their phone lines and rural power poles cut with storms. Give me darkness. I will fight my way out. Give me light. I will seek to cover it.

The department head called me into his office. I sat across from him with books to the ceiling and stacks of papers crosswise on his desk, his file cabinets open, and papers even piled up on the floor. My own office felt less cluttered when I sat in his. Behind him, a large window opened to the campus where I saw students walking between classes. Through the upper limbs of the large tree outside Old Main, I could see the chapel and the buildings farther away on the quadrangle. There had been complaints about my teaching, he said. Was I doing enough prep work? Did I have lesson plans? Did I need a mentor? The department head paused, and I realized he was waiting for my answers to his many questions. Didn't he know I began to hear voices and wanted to follow them? They were not in my ears, no, but in my imagination. Didn't he know I had to find the ocean from which they called, or they would be gone? Didn't he know I had to save the voices from drowning, age after age, as they had always done? Hadn't he told me I needed publication?

What was wrong with the students? Couldn't they pick up a log now and then? Couldn't they take the boat out? Relieve the pressure of academia on my neck. In my throat. Yes, I would be prepared next class. I tied a rag around my mouth to keep my voice from screeching. I put a harness on the voices to hold them back while I wrote notes for classes.

I was not used to the gravity. Was there gravity in the ocean? I was used to wandering in the imagination. Now I had to think. What would I say about the assigned text?

I heard them mumble. Who were they? Not the students. No. But the voices I heard. They were voices of women. Women from a long time ago. Why did they bother me? Go away. There's another house down the road. They don't lock their doors.

A Chapter in Which the Beginning Begins to Shred

My colleagues knew I was in trouble. They looked at me with their eyes hitting against each other like boats too near the shore. I had tenure review coming. Did I want to be replaced by another? What was I to do? Be a soldier on some field following a general after his own rules? Or did I want to be adrift on the great sea of academia, spending my time looking for another position? But I had served on significant committees and had built a presence at the college. I had led prayer at several convocations. I looked to colleagues in other departments for backing.

I wanted to hear the voices speak. I drew them near. At night, I dried them with a paper towel. I put them in a bowl. They were clams in their shells. I put a blanket over them. I told them not to worry.

The storm drove me to an outpost of myself. I worried that I wouldn't have strength to fight. I was still in the blizzard of the night when I woke. I remembered driving through a blizzard once, my husband at the wheel, the children in the backseat, headlights on the snow aiming for the car. Incoming snow from the bomber clouds. My thoughts storming my head.

Should I go to more conferences? Deliver more papers on my research? And what was my research, other than the voices I heard? Nothing, I suppose. They had taken over. Yes, I would concentrate on teaching. Push the voices aside like so many papers I had to grade.

HISPERA

Noah's Wife

A Chapter Floating on the Water

LATE ONE SEMESTER, I made a short trip to a conference in Anchorage. At the Alaska Native Heritage Center, I found an old story of the flood passed down by Ivisaaa and Uivaqsaat at Umiat Inupiat:

> Long ago the earth was flooded.
>
> People hunted sea mammals but stayed in their kayaks all the time.
>
> One day they saw a tussock of grass floating in the water.
>
> Raven speared it and the ocean began to recede and the tussock became the Arctic coastal plain.
>
> —Elijah Kakinya and Simon Paneak, *Nunamiut Unipkaanich Nunamiut Stories*

Then, driving on I-70 through the mountains of eastern Utah, I listened to a woman on *NPR* talk about Noah during his journey in the ark. "What was it like?" they asked her.

"Noah didn't speak," she answered, "He didn't sleep." What was she talking about? It didn't seem that way to me. Noah spoke. He slept in the rocking of the ark over the floodwaters. His labor of building finally over. It was a respite for him, though he had animals to feed and stables to clean. The animals also made their noises as they floated in semi-hibernation. It was Noah's wife I heard in the rock facings along I-70. She was there in her tunic, her apron, with a cloth covering her head. It was night as I drove through the Utah mountains. And cold—only twenty-five degrees. The full moon made ghostly walls of the rock escarpments. I felt suspended above the earth. The mountains somehow like water.

She was sort of milquetoasty,
a shadowy figure lugging sacks of oats up the plank.
—Denise Duhamel, "Noah and Joan"

...and the earth was filled with violence.
—Gen 6:11

In the beginning of the ark, there are piles of cut trees in the yard. Often, I look away. It is a pattern I call rubble. Noah won't listen to reason. He won't answer my questions. Years and years he works.

Three of our sons, Ham, Shem, and Japheth, get in line with Noah. The daughters-in-law, Karisha, Ruleah, and Rishon, somehow agree—they would build an ark. God commanded it. How many times does it seem no progress is made? Just Noah and our sons felling gopher trees.

Marauders make off with some of the lumber. Noah and our sons cut more trees and drag them behind the donkeys to our yard. All of them sleep now at the ark, which is nothing but a pile of lumber. Sometimes people gather to watch. I hear their laughter as I prepare meals. Yet the large scaffolding begins to take shape, until the outline of the ark overshadows our house.

Now the men work inside the ark, building three stories. Noah tells me to prepare parchments. I ask, "What for?" He doesn't answer, but tells me to stock the pantry shelves. My daughters-in-law and I gather seeds, herbs, roots, grains. We pack jars, bundles, baskets. We carry into the pantry whatever we can—dried, smoked, or preserved in salt. We stack hay for the animals. We prepare buckets for water that will soon be gone. "They won't be enough," I tell Noah. "What will we do for the rest of the water we need?"

They build a large door for the ark. They seal the cracks with pitch.

Strange animals gather two-by-two at the edge of our yard. I understand the camels, horses, cattle, sheep, goats, rabbits, ducks. Even the deer, caribou, buffalo, bear. But lemurs, scorpions, snakes, skunks? Each day,

Uprising of Goats

I'm astonished at the gathering: lizard, gnu, aardvark, hyena, caterpillar, ostrich, penguin, giraffe, hippopotamus, walrus, cheetah, zebra, armadillo, hedgehog. Where did they come from? What is their purpose?

Each morning, there are more of them. It's the animals that haunt me. They come without knowing how to come. Without our bidding, they arrive as though they should be here.

"I don't want to go," I tell Noah.

He takes my hand. "Get in the ark. Otherwise you'll drown."

"I can't leave my sheep," I say.

"The ark, Hispera."

"Take the aardvarks out. The tub of walruses. Make room for my sheep."

Noah raises his stick—

Just how does one hear God? How does one get on his side? It's not where I want to be.

"Obedience," Noah says.

I watch the animals enter the ark. Noah guides them to their pens and latches the gates.

My sons and daughters-in-law enter the ark. No one else wants to come. The door is closed. We sit there. We sit there. We sit. We sit. Seven days. I should have cut lavender to hold under our noses. I cry over my little flock of sheep. I would have left, but the door is sealed and there is no escape. We hear the taunting of the people. We hear the thud of rocks thrown at the ark. I can't look at my daughters-in-law. I hear their little cryings. Their little angers. The arguments in the corner they try to cover. Rishon decides she wants out, but it's too late.

We hear a sound in the distance. A rumbling—as if... What? A sound I've never heard. I have nothing to compare it to. *Ssshhhheeeeeeeeerrrrr* . . . Sheets of water must be sweeping over the ark. More rumbling. More streaks of light. More questioning from the animals. The little squeals of the monkeys are pitiful. It is a kind of water I do not know. Not a bucket or two from the well, but from some deep wellspring in the earth. And from the sky. Rain, Noah calls it. Thunder and lightning. It gives him a chance to name. It is falling because God is mad at the people he made. They have disappointed him.

Even the lightning has a smell.

I want to touch the animals to quiet them. But Noah won't let me. We can't interfere with the return to their way of life. The animals will face dormancy and hibernation, Noah says. A time of withdrawal. Of endurance. Yes, there will be much of that. Noah says they'll settle down. But not yet.

We feel the ark wobble. We know it has come loose from the ground. We stumble one way, then the other.

"Hold on," Noah says to us. The ark rocks back and forth, hitting against trees as it moves. We have to hold on to the center posts. The natting of the goats nearly sounds like laughter. The daughters-in-law cry. Rishon is sick, throwing up in her apron. My son, Japeth, cannot help her because of the unsteady rocking. We would be tossed if we let go of the posts.

"Stay on the floor," Japeth says. "Keep your head down." But she tumbles back and forth.

I would have preferred my daughters to my daughters-in-law.

Noah tells us the ark will level. I cower when I see the flashing lights and hear the noise. Somehow, the flashes seep into the ark—and the noise. But not the water. Who is this God who would drown a frightened flock of sheep? We follow a God who can cause rain and then fix the broken sky, Noah assures me. The sound of rain pours over the roof of the ark. I think at first it is wind, and it is, but wind with the sweeping water. My daughters-in-law and I hide in our hammocks with the sound of rain and dry heaves. The noise of the great opening of the waters roars in our ears. I think the ark will tip over and float upside down in the waves, leaving us flailing against one another on the ceiling of the ark, which will become the floor.

In the beginning of travel, we swim like fish large as the first month of floating. It is as God wishes it to be. It is not what I wish. It is getting used to what someone else wants. It is the story we know who are women. It is my own will that moves in the night. I could think it was the animals, but I know they're the arguments I have against God. What happened is not what I would have made happen. I still would have my sheep, and not all these animals that stir in their places with complaints that are my own. Sometimes I listen to their voices. I think they grieve the loss of their kind outside the ark.

Now we must be above the trees, for we no longer hit anything. Billows of air come in the roof-window when it is opened, as though the billows are passengers also. But gusts of rain fall into the ark too, and Noah has our sons close the window. Even the animals stir with the new smell in their noses.

There are times when the elephants sway back and forth until I think they will topple the ark. Noah tells them to be still. They have to stay in their cages. We have to have order. We all have to stay in our places until the flood passes. Once the tiger growls, as though warning the elephants to stand still. Then I have to warn the tiger, who is the main pacer: back and forth, back and forth. "Don't you get dizzy?" I ask at its cage.

In the night, someone is tossing. A son or daughter-in-law. I think of our other children. Daughters and sons-in-law who chose their own way. They couldn't tolerate a father with an ark in the yard—or the whole town laughing as they passed by our house to gawk.

I listen to the animals rooting in the straw two floors above us. Their noises are my dreams. I look at their faces. At the eyes that look back me, two-by-two, when I comfort them with my words.

Maybe it is Noah, still tossing as he did for all those years during the building. What can be troubling him? His work is over. His vision came to pass. We had been outcasts, laughed at during the building of the ark. What's different about this journey? How is it that God spoke to Noah? How did he know about the flood? Why did God choose him? Even the animals seemed to know when it was time to enter the ark.

There's a terrible darkness inside the ark that I can touch with my hand. Noah keeps a coal burning in a hanging bucket. He keeps up the fire. He has to have power over something. After the first terrible days of tossing, I ask if I can burn the little oil lamp. I have to see into the pantry where our provisions are stored—where Noah tied them after my daughters-in-law and I finished our work of loading. Somewhere in the darkness, we have light.

In the beginning of our silence, I hear the little slap of waves against the corners of the ark. I hear Shem and Ham or Japeth letting down the buckets to fill with water. Dragging them up again on the end of the rope. I hear them walking among the feeding and water troughs with their buckets and shovels and tools. I find comfort in the hammocks. The rocking. The robes covering us. We find little to say to one another during those first fearful days of our exile. I wake in the morning crying for the sheep I left behind. Sometimes I think I hear their *baaa*. Maybe it comes from my own mouth.

It would be colder in the ark, but for the heat of the animals. The sturdier ones—the animals with heavy fur—have cages along the inside walls of the ark, where it is colder. The frailer animals are closer to the center, where it is warm. I ask Noah if I can move the wombats, for they seem to be shivering whenever I pass their cage. He agrees. I exchange their cage with that of the beavers, who grumble at the disturbance.

Noah calls me to the roof window. I see the waters that cover the earth. Nothing but water under the sky. I cry at the sight of it. My daughters-in-law sob. Even Noah has a look on his face I've not seen before. We have been spared the drowning of the earth. It seems a harsh punishment to me. Did my little flock of sheep gather at the ark when we were inside? I hear their bleating, I tell Noah. O flock. My little flock. The clouds over us look like lamb's fleece. He takes my hand. I see the sorrow on his face. Maybe he is thinking of the donkeys that brayed after they pulled the heavy trees for the ark. No, he is thinking of the people—the children and relatives.

Once in a while, the clear sky can be seen from the ark, though it still rains. Sometimes we see the stars again at night through the clouds. At least they did not drown.

There is horrendous solitude. "Where is everyone?" Ruleah asks one day, and she cries the rest of the afternoon, though Shem tries to comfort her. I hear other little arguments and disgruntlements that my sons and daughters-in-law try to keep quiet. Heated words they try to whisper. Their little conversations rise to a frantic pitch they can't keep to themselves.

Sometimes the animals pick it up and seem to fuss until Noah walks among them. Other times they hum and talk to themselves. I like the sounds of the little goats. If my children were as obedient as them . . .

The water is unimaginable. It sways like the elephants did as they walked into the ark, their long trunks sweeping back and forth. The waves move something like the elephants—when the elephants walk—when they are not caged.

At first, the smoke from the little oil lamp and the cooking pot alarms the animals. But the roof-window pulls the smoke up and out into the open, wet air.

Often, we don't have a fire. I press lentil cakes and unwrap figs.

The animals make sounds at certain times of the day. It becomes a routine. Some are restless at night. Others are restless in the morning. Still others remain in a stupor. They hardly eat the hay we put into their pens. The birds peck at the grain I place in their cages. "Someday we will be able to leave," I tell them. Look at them. More obedient than people.

There are times I felt restlessness rise in my bones. My family feels it. The animals feel it too. I soothe them with my words. "It will soon be over,"

I say. They will have land under their feet again. They will return to what they know.

But will they? What will remain of what we knew when the waters abate? Isn't that the purpose of the flood? To destroy what had been?

How shrill is the elephant's call, as if crying to God, asking the reason for the suspension of its life over these waters. Or maybe it is praise to God for its life.

Yes, we have that. Noah prays in the mornings and evenings, praising the God of our survival. I think sometimes he prays all day. We sit with him. I have my knitting. I make socks for our cold feet. I make a shawl for Rishon, who always seems to be shivering, like the wombat. I think the animals are praying also. Often they are quiet, or if there is a noise, they seem to join our prayers with their lowing and humming. Sometimes they sound nearly human. Sometimes I climb the little walkways between the stalls in the upper stories just to have somewhere to go.

Noah keeps a journal of our journey on the water. He keeps the parchments rolled up on the shelves in his study in the ark—his library. They are skins on which the number of the days of our trip is marked: it rained forty days and forty nights, and now we are floating. The journal is written on the goatskins he asked me to dry and tan before our "voyage," the name Noah gives to our constant moving. That's the reason for the parchments he wanted. He thought of writing even before we were on the ark. My daughters-in-law asked me why we were bringing them even as they helped me carry the rolled-up animal skins up to his shelves. The measurements of the ark are also stored here, along with the older parchments that contain our genealogies and the histories that have been passed down through the generations.

In the beginning of our time without rain, Noah continues to write. I see how writing is a voyage for him. He says his words are about what he thinks. Mainly, he keeps a record of forage. When we are nearing the end of it, the voyage will be over, because he followed God's instructions in building the storage bins.

The words we speak have light in them. But the words Noah writes are solid—a rock to rest against in a distant pasture. That's what the written word is. A solid boat on the sheer light of a wide sea.

One day, we hear terrible winds. Noah says they are blowing the water back into the earth and up into the sky. One evening, he opens the window of the ark, and the moon has lighted the water.

Noah's Wife

"I think the moon once was covered with water," I tell Noah. Now it roams the sky. It doesn't have to stay in a wooden cave.

One day, we feel the ark hit something solid. Something not water! We are startled. It bumps again. Karisha falls, then turns over an empty bucket.

"Hold on to her," Noah says to Ham. The ark hits *solid* again. For several days we feel the bumping. Then, from the window, we see land jutting up out of the water. "A mountain," Noah says. Noah, the namer of what we see.

"It looks more like a hill," Shem says.

"No, higher," Noah says.

"How far are we from home?" Karisha asks.

I'm afraid the boat will topple down the mountain-side with all the animals in it. How will we get them out? The ark keeps bumping. The daughters-in-law cry, "Is there a pole to push the ark away?"

"You can't push a huge ark," Noah says. "We have weight in here." The ark skids, bump by bump. The animals bray and make sounds of alarm. Then, just as suddenly, the ark stands solid and upright on firm ground. It is quiet as we wait to see if the ark will slip again. The animals listen in silence. There, in the distance, the sound of water receding down the mountain. We wait seven more days. We wait. We wait. We wait.

One day, Noah opens the window of the ark to let one of the birds fly away—a crow—which we never see again. Then the dove he let loose comes huffing back. The next dove does not.

Noah leaves the window open now. We wait seven days again. He marks them on the parchment. Then Noah and our sons open the door. With a great banging it comes loose. They lower it to the ground. Bright light floods the ark. The world is all *shiny*. Noah falls to his knees. The daughters-in-law cry with relief, then howl with sorrow that their families are not there to meet them. I cry for my children—and my sheep that are not there. Noah opens the pens and the animals begin to leave the ark. I reach out to them—*don't leave*.

The animals walk stiffly, like the little clay animals the boys used to play with. I want to stay on the ark. I pull back from the hand Noah offers me. I shade my eyes against the bright sun, looking back into the ark. What is ahead of us but this soggy ground? Where is the world we knew?

A Chapter in Which Things Start to Go Bad between Us

THE FIRE WAS NOT his fault. I was in the kitchen when I heard the spigot squeak on. Then I saw the flames. I heard them crackle like breaking twigs and the call of a neighbor trying to interrupt the spreading blaze. I smelled the smoke. I dried my hands and ran from the house. The fire crawled across the yard as if a wind from a giant bellows had picked it up. There was nothing we could do to stop it. The garage and the corner of the house were in flames before we heard the sirens. The garden hose was a garter snake against it.

I tell you, you never know what worms are in the can you open. The can is deeper than you think. I promise you, the cut from a can-lid leaves a jagged scar.

What were you doing? What were you thinking? I was angry. I was horrified at our loss. Who would have to fill out the insurance forms? Who would have to find another place for us to stay? Who would have to handle everything that was not my fault? The great inconvenience at the beginning of an academic year. How could I console the girls on the loss of their possessions? How could I console myself?

He was trying to burn off a hornet's nest from the corner of the garage, he said. I hadn't even known it was there.

I tried to forgive him. I couldn't forget. I held it against him, and there was nothing I could do but turn away. How could I trust him when he had burned more than half of our house away? The rest could not be saved. Smoke and water damage. The wet mattresses. The sofa and chairs. The

A Chapter in Which Things Start to Go Bad between Us

charred timbers. The hard clumps of insulation sticking out of the walls. The strings of tar hanging from the roof. There was a way to treat furniture with a chemical that would take away the smell of smoke, but it was always there. I could smell it on my skin and in my hair. Sometimes when I returned to my office after a class, I could smell a whiff of the smoke I had left.

I didn't want to be with him. I grew more distant. Distrustful. Anger lingered like a buzzing nest. It was the way his father had gotten rid of bees and wasps. He remembered standing beside his father, both of them finally running from the angry insects. Our church gathered around us. We were active in our church. The adult Bible study. I saw a vision of the flames of hell. They were inside my own head. They were directed at Walker. Our insurance paid for two hotel rooms while we looked for another house. I couldn't sleep in the same bed with him. I asked for a room with two beds. I would have slept in our daughter's room, but each wanted their own bed. I lay in bed at night stifled with anger. Was it now hatred? Both Walker and I had lost our offices in the house. I had backed up my work at my office in the religious studies department, though not all my research was covered. Nor were my books, a few of which I'd had since I was in college. Why had I left myself vulnerable? Why had I married? Why had I not known he would bring the house down on our heads? What had they ever done but burn down our houses? I sat in the pastor's office. He read passages on forgiveness. Walker and I counseled together as man and wife. Better or worse. I continued our sessions with crying I could not stop. Once, near the end, after one raging argument, Walker said he had discovered who the real hornet was. He moved into the new house with us, but he did not stay long.

Bless the thread of work that stitches up the gapping places. Bless the voices that had known betrayal. When I worked on the voices, I could leave my own life and think about another even more lonely and displaced than mine, and in doing that, I could come back to my own life, comfort my daughters, and help them look ahead to college. Walker and I had toured colleges with them. We had liked our road trips. It was our last time as a family. The girls had decided on a college in another state. They were ready to reach out to places they had not been. The loss of a house and all its belongings, the breakup of a twenty-year marriage, the imagined voices of biblical women who had not been given space in the Bible to tell their side. How could I not be preoccupied?

HAGAR

The Little Goat Trail
A Chapter in Which Land Appears

I took with me Hagar, the little Egyptian slave girl. What trouble could she be?
—Sarai, Gen 16:1

Here I speak. A bell around my neck. "What's the purpose?" I ask. Someone wants to know where I am?

I saw them with their sheep and goats. They came to Egypt from the desert. We watched them from the window of Pharaoh's house. I saw the way they walked. Their flocks were jumpy. Yet the herders drew them in, not cruelly, but wanting them near. They had not always wandered in the desert. I saw their garments. They were not dusty and wrinkled like desert wanderers. What would it be like to go where I wanted?

I saw the men look at her. She was old, yet men wanted her. She said she was a sister of the man she traveled with. I thought it was plain she was his wife. But Pharaoh took her into his house. I was given to her. A slave girl of no account. I did what she said. I combed her hair and washed her clothes and brought her food. No one cared what I wanted.

Pharaoh would have taken her as a wife, but something happened. He was sick and the soothsayers must have said, she's the man's wife.

The Little Goat Trail

Pharaoh sent them away. She took me with them—with all their flocks and herds, their cattle, sheep, goats, donkeys, camels—and all the people with them. Some were slaves. Some were family. It was hard to tell.

I AM LEAVING EGYPT. I am going to the dust storms in the desert. Sometimes we walk. Sometimes we ride camels. We are going across the desert! We camped and I was afraid of the night. I shivered. I saw men guarding animals. I watched the stars across the sky. Yes, I was going too—away from Egypt. I WILL DO WHAT I WANT TO DO.

She had no children. She was sorry. There were times I came from milking goats and saw her heaviness.

It was her idea. Not mine. She called me to the tent. What was it now? I slept with Abram until a child was conceived. But when she saw I conceived, she struck me. When she raised her hand again, I ran from her. I could go where I wanted. Not back to Egypt—though it was better than desert tents with the smell of animals. I could stay between rocks, or shelter beneath bushes. What would I do at night when animals growled? There always were places in slave quarters to hide. There were places in Pharaoh's house. A small hidden place within the larger place. I WOULD MAKE MY OWN RULES. They would not tell me what to do.

I was thirsty and found a spring of water. What if there were robbers or herders nearby? But no one saw me. Who would notice? I walked toward a hill, but it remained far in the distance. Where did I have to go? WHO WOULD CARE WHAT HAPPENED TO ME? They have tents, and Pharoah has all of Egypt. I have nothing!

Then I heard a Voice: *Hagar, slave girl, where have you come from?* I looked to see who spoke.

"I am running from Sarai," I answered to the one who was as invisible as me.

The Voice told me to return to Sarai. I felt bitter tears. I ran again, but his voice stopped me. The Voice I could not see or really hear, but it was there—inside: *I will multiply your offspring such that they cannot be counted for the multitude. You have conceived and will bear a son. You will call his name, Ishmael, for the lord has heard your affliction.*

What followed was the hard news: *He will be a wild man, with his hand against everyone, and everyone's hand against him* (Gen 16:12).

Hadn't I known that in Egypt? I was the slave of a slave, sent away with strangers from palace to desert. Why did I have so hard a life while Sarai sat in Abram's tent, loved by him?

But I listened to the Voice that spoke to me. I called him El-Roi.[1] Had I really seen God and remained alive?

I returned to Abram's camp. I heard the sheep and goats. The noisy little groups always talked to one another. They lived together without slaves. No, I have seen the animals butt one another. I've seen their cruelty to the weaker. Little slave animals.

I stayed to myself, away from Sarai. Then one night, Ishmael was born. I saw that Abram loved him.

Then SHE was going to have a child. The child promised to her in her old age, she said. Finally, the HE, the ISAAC, was born. I held Ishmael the night I heard her cries. The favored one is here. The younger one who will replace us.

Ishmael played with Isaac, and SHE saw it. I called him away, but it was too late. "Cast out the slave woman and her son," I heard Sarai say.

The Voice, El-Roi, spoke to Abram. I could tell by Abram's face when he looked at me. He was not distressed, but let us go. *I will make a nation of Ishmael because he is your offspring* (Gen 21:12–13).

Wasn't it HER idea in the first place? Now it was HER idea that we go. AND WHERE WOULD WE GO? Into the wilderness, with the wild beasts and vagrants and wanderers? Let herself go be there with El-Roi, who was agreeing with her also. But hadn't I wanted to go on my own? To make what I wanted to make with my own hands?

Abram put a skin of water over my shoulder and handed me some bread wrapped in cloth. I couldn't carry Ishmael. He was too big. We started into the wilderness. When the water was gone, and the bread too, I left Ishmael under one of the bushes. I went away from him because I didn't want to see him die from thirst. I would have gone farther, but I heard El-Roi speak: *Go, lift him up and take his hand.*

I was alone in the desert, yet I heard his Voice. Would his Voice keep the wild beasts away? I knew he was there. But he was an invisible he.

We came upon desert tribes. Ishmael and I traveled with them as they moved from well to well with their flocks. I milked the goats, wove their hair into cloth for the tents, and tended the flocks as I had learned to do in the desert. I kept my head covered. I stayed out of the way of other women. I had had enough of them. I wanted to be invisible. I felt sometimes the hand of El-Roi covered me. Was he anything other than a Voice?

---

1. "God hears."

The Little Goat Trail

I told Ishmael about Abram, his father. I told him he was the son of one favored by El-Roi. I told him not to tell the others. Ishmael had the mark of a leader upon him. He belonged to the God of Abram, who left us abandoned in the desert. Did Abram ever wonder what happened to us? Did he send a stranger out once in a while to find us? Did the stranger return to Abram and tell him where we were? DID ABRAM EVER WANT US BACK? I don't think he thought about us.

Ishmael grew. It wasn't long before he began to take wives. He wanted to wander on his own. I argued with Ishmael, but I did what he wanted. We left the tribes we had lived with and became our own tribe.

Soon Ishmael had many sons: Nebajoth and Kedar, Adbeel and Mibsam, Mishma and Dumah, Massa and Hadad, Tema and Jetur, Naphish and Kedemah (Gen 25:13–15). When they were grown, they parted from us with their families.

Look at my offspring spread across the desert. Imagine, a slave girl as the mother of a nation. Imagine us at your heels—like the stars of heaven.

Ishmael Had a Box of Crayons

When I went through the rubble of our burned house, I found some childhood drawings my girls had made. The corners of the drawings were singed, but a few of them could be saved. There was also an old box of their crayons, melted together in a clump, the way our lives stuck together until they were separated under pressure with the sound of a crack.

The crayon marks were beasts. The crayons made marks like desert shrubs. They were a billow of smoke. They spoke in my will. I didn't speak for them. They spoke for me. My words carried spirits. My words wore bandanas on their heads like desert warriors. To will. To will. I am consumed. I am consumed. A burning bush that burned. A whirlwind. A dock on a churning lake. A web of duct tape. An open hole. A willingness to write the voices I heard. To be a conduit. Why did they think I was in religious studies? But how far would it stretch? To the ends of the earth, I once thought. To the fiery pits of hell.

The fire could not keep us warm. The fire was too small. The fire was a risk. They would know where we were. The asteroids were clinking at the edge of the water. We let the splashes douse the fire. In darkness we became ourselves, fearful of the light that would show us who we were.

I sent the pieces about Hispera and Hagar out for publication. I received them back. I continued writing. I continued preparing my lectures. I began praying for tenure—for my preparation for tenure.

At first the voices were far away. I didn't think anything of them. They were like filaments, or fragments. Neighbors talking in the backyard, or a radio playing somewhere. I couldn't understand them at first. Other noises accompanied them from time to time: the bells from the church in the distance, or the birds in a tree.

I was aware of the noises. They were somehow connected to the voices that were waiting to be heard—that had been calling for a long time. I've always been interested in voices that did not have a chance to speak—voices that have been on the outside—maybe because I've felt that way. One day as I walked, a car of passing boys actually barked.

I didn't talk to anyone about the possibilities of presenting the voices. I wanted to embed them in the parallel happenings of academic life. The classroom interrupted by scholarship, and scholarship interrupted by creative work, and creative work interrupted by students calling, and students calling interrupted by meetings between faculty, the department, committees and sub-committees, and the reports due afterwards. I always had something to do that got in the way of what I wanted to do, and what I wanted to do got in the way of what I had to do. Everything was done with less effort than I should have put into it, because one task pulled concentration and energy away from the other.

There were times I was aware of this other world—this *beyond*, if that was the term. Maybe it was because I was aging and beginning to think of what came next. I wanted to see the old voices' relevance to contemporary life. I wanted to present the marginalized voices, to present the struggle for equilibrium on academic and creative levels, and within the creative frame, present the bifurcation of working with my own voice and with the voices of others so far away.

I felt the voices had been waiting for someone to become aware of them. I was in my office at my desk when I distinctly heard another voice: *I want to have my hands in the threads. I want to sew.* I typed those words. Others followed. Then there were changes and rearrangements of words. Notes in the margins of my lecture notes. It's not that I minded the voices, but I tried to keep my mind on my lectures. I had to know what I was doing. I couldn't walk into class and talk about the voices I heard.

I prepared my lectures diligently. I often spent hours writing them, though they took less than an hour to give. Others could walk into any classroom and talk to the end of the hour, or to the end of three hours if it were a seminar. I had to know what I was going to say. I had to know where the class was going. How could a lecture that took so long to write take less than an hour to give? Sometimes much less, because I always left time for questions. I also spent hours preparing exams, though it only took the students an hour to answer them. Then I spent more hours grading the exams and making appropriate comments.

The imagined voices of these biblical women kept complicating the situation. I decided to give in. I closed the door of my office and continued with the first voice—the one that wanted to sew, though there were certainly other voices, several at least. But I decided that I had to focus. I felt everything would connect, eventually, but for now it would be one voice at a time. I continued to write, though students knocked on my door with questions about their papers, or their majors, or anything they wanted to talk about. Who were these voices? I thought, as a student asked how many course were required for a religion minor. Before the door closed, I had turned back to my computer.

Why were the voices angry? Maybe not angry. But disgruntled. Their voices were a protest against their circumstances. They spoke an uprising against silence. Maybe it was my voice I was hearing, filtered through theirs. There was loneliness in the academic life. The striving for tenure. Watching every move. Looking suspiciously at students who might give poor teaching evaluations that would hurt me and hurt my chances for tenure. There were bears waiting under my desk. Wolverines in the corners of the room. Packs of wolves. Foxes. Herds of caribou. A dark cloud hovered on the ceiling, waiting to rain. There were unseen beings surrounding the walls. Blizzards on the horizon. There was a shouting for attention. Justine Crowd was the leader of the see-me-shine movement within the department. An article published here. A book review there. I am going to a conference to give a paper. I am an adjudicator for a recognized journal. A group of students have asked me to let them into my class even though it is full.

It was the goats I heard. Surely the women I heard were familiar with goats. They tended them, milked them, wove goat-hair garments, tanned their hides for writing parchment. The goat was an animal of service, as overlooked as women.

I went to another conference I had not planned on attending, nor had I made arrangements with the college to finance the trip. I needed to boost my list of conferences for tenure review. There were several changes in flights, and I missed the last flight back. Walker agreed to visit the girls on Parents' Day. The department head said he would take my classes for the day. Probably to inquire about whether I had improved my teaching.

Ishmael Had a Box of Crayons

    I made notes for my tenure application as I sat in the airport. I knew other voices of biblical women would come. How would I include them in scholarship? How long had they waited for someone to listen? Sometimes the voices shifted. I couldn't remember which one came first. I could see them in a row as the line of passengers waiting to board the plane. Each one carried a spirit within them.

Walker hoped for a reconciliation. The girls argued for it. The pastor of our church counseled me on my own. Was my crisis with Walker a crisis with God? Had the fire uncovered an alienation from God? I didn't know. Had it? I had always gone to church. I had always heard God's voice through Scripture. I loved the upheaval of the Red Sea. The opening up of the earth and the swallowing of the rebellious ones (Num 16:28–34). I had felt comfort in being an obedient believer. What had I done? But my dreams were nightmares. Was it pressure from my classes? My preparations for tenure? My own insecurity? The plea from other believers that divorce was not God's recommendation? The barb of Justine Crowd, a colleague? The evil intent in my own evil heart?

Maybe I felt God move out of the house. Maybe I moved out of his. No, our church believed in blessed assurance. A child of God could run away, but still remained a child. As the college moved toward a more fundamental stance, I felt the stretch marks. I had to make a statement of faith for the opening of my letter for tenure. That statement would dictate the application I was writing.

DORCAS

The Closets of Heaven
A Chapter in Which Fabric Is a Weighty Matter

Now there was at Joppa a disciple named Tabitha, which by interpretation is called Dorcas, or gazelle, who was full of good works and almsdeeds which she did.

And it came to pass, she was sick and died; whom, when they had washed, laid in an upper chamber.

And as Lydda was near to Joppa, and the disciples heard that Peter was there, they sent two men, asking him to come.

They brought him into the upper chamber; and all the widows stood by him weeping, and showing the coats and garments Dorcas made.

But Peter put them all forth, and kneeled down, and prayed; and turning to the body said, Tabitha, arise. And she opened her eyes; and when she saw Peter, she sat up.

And he gave her his hand, and lifted her up; and when he had called the saints and widows, presented her alive.

And it was known throughout Joppa; and many believed in the Lord.

And it came to pass that he stayed many days in Joppa with Simon, a tanner.

—Acts 9:36–43

The Closets of Heaven

What sort of miracles did he perform, that preacher, he said, turning to the women, and what did he preach about, for that matter?
—Pär Lagerkvist, *Barabbas*

then updraft seized, gravity winnowed, the falling raggedly
reversed, depth suddenly pursued ...
—Jorie Graham, "Thinking"

I

Dorcas' Life

I ONLY WANT TO sew, to have my hands in the threads.

I watch the waves at Joppa stitch the shore. I move my needle like the sea where ships wash to the shore as we are washed into this life. I think we live to do something for someone else. I'm always sewing for others, but it's because I love to feel the needle pull thread through the cloth. Sewing is my prayer. The head is my centurion, not the heart.

The *euangelista* have been to Joppa. They said how Jesus suffered, how he was alone on the cross between the two men. But he kept his head.

I sew my garments with the other women. They come to my house; I listen to their words. We talk about Jesus. We hear that some of his disciples are writing down what he did and said, each one saying it in his own way. There are new Scriptures in the making. I want to say, "In the sewing."

Jesus left upheaval where he walked. There is argument and disagreement everywhere. He called himself the Son of God. He said he was the only way to God, yet our shore is full of gods.

"How did Jesus rise from the dead?"

"Did he rise?" some ask.

"How can we know what happened?"

Even his believers have different ways of believing in contradiction to one another. I hear them as I finger the cloth in the marketplace. The shadows of the palm tree move across the rolls of linen as if sewing them.

Jesus was a storm off the sea, a Zealot, drifting us apart.

Dorcas' Life

In the marketplace, I hear those who don't believe. They are the Epicureans and Stoics. There is a philosophy for everyone. There is a god for everyone. But all points seem in reaction to Jesus. I hear his name wherever I go.

The women seem to be the first to believe, yet they do not speak openly. The men don't have to hide what they believe.

The Sadducees and Pharisees argue in the heat.

The Gentiles say they have been adopted by the God of Israel because they believe Jesus was the son of God.

The Jews stop arguing among themselves and set their teeth against them.

The Gentiles are as left out as if they were women.

We hear from Jerusalem that the Christians meet in the catacombs. There are persecutions. There are floggings and other crucifixions. Some of the women cry while we sew. Sometimes we jump at a noise as if someone were coming. Jesus is the Savior. We choose to believe, though others say both he and his upheaval will pass.

When the sky is pale, it is a linen tunic. But in the evening, the tunic is wool, draping its blues and reds across the sea.

We hear from Jerusalem that some people in an upper room began speaking in languages not their own. They spoke in tongues, we heard. Whatever that meant. It was another burden for the mystery of what we heard.

I walk to the fish markets and the street markets where other languages come with the laughter from other places. The city catches the light from across the sea. I walk between the boats and rows of fish and piles of net as I listen to the voices of the fishermen. There is Simon, the *burseus*,[1] in his oxhide sandals. My sandals are made of palm-bark bound to my feet with thongs.

I live in a house with an upper room and a flat roof with stone steps leading up to it from a dusty street. It is like all the other houses with their perrons. I hear the hooves of a donkey clatter over the few places where there are cobblestones. They are uneven, uncertain. Sometimes I see the donkeys as little boats on the shore.

---

1. "Tanner."

Uprising of Goats

I have a pitcher of water at the door, which I pour over my feet to keep the dust from the sheen of the hard, earthen floor.

Sometimes a child stands at my door.

"Dorcas."

"What do you want?" I ask.

"I want to sew."

The women pray for Joppa as our needles push the shore of the cloth. The landscape is lovely, rolling toward the sea. The city is full of good works. The olive orchards shimmer. Everything is as it should be.

The garments we make are *chitones*, *pepla*, and *himatia*. They are tunics of different lengths, fastened at the shoulders and tied with a sash around the waist with fullness at the front and back. Sometimes they're embroidered, sometimes brocaded, sometimes quilted.

I can't remember the first time I felt the little pain. I think nothing of it. But I feel it. Maybe it is from sitting too long in my chair. I move closer to the light. Sometimes my eyes hurt. My body is stiff.

After the crucifixion, Jesus was seen alive. The dead have been raised. The sick have been healed.

For me, it was the way Jesus thought. "We don't live by bread alone," he said (Matt 4:4). "But by the act of sewing," I think he should have said.

After Jesus' death, Judas hanged himself.

A man took the money Judas got for the betrayal of Jesus and bought a field with it.

Betrayal has its cost.

So does faith.

We also hear that after Jesus' death, Peter arranged for another disciple, Matthias, to take the place of Judas. Peter is always arranging, always fishing from the shore.

I hear the new believers sell their possessions and share things in common. I would not do that.

Sometimes we share our silence as we work.

I see the girl still standing at my door. "I want to sew," she says.

She is like the ocean with a ship on it. A desert with a camel.

I feel sometimes I walk like a camel. The joint on my foot has given way and my large toe crosses over the smaller ones. My foot throbs in my sandals. Both my mother's feet were that way; I remember asking if they hurt.

I get impatient with the women who come to my house to sew. "What do I do now?" they ask.

My needle embroiders the cloth. I don't want to stop. I don't want to decide what they should do. When I sew, my needle is a sparrow taking a dust bath.

I am glad when the women leave. I chase the girl away. I watch the blue sky disappear in its reddest corner. I like my own thoughts. I think sometimes they are an oar.

The man and woman are arguing again in the next house. I hear them as I light the fire for my olive oil and barley cake in the evening.

I come from two worlds: Greek and Hebrew. I come from two other worlds: faith and works.

I have a house; I am not poor. I sew for others. Whatever is done is done for good. It is done for history.

History is a gazelle; it runs by quickly. It's as though Jesus was just on earth, but now he's gone. It's as if I was a girl, but now I'm an old woman. It's as if I was just married, but now I'm a widow.

History is an animal. Standing. Running. Sleeping. Killing. Then it is gone. But other histories are born. They are always there. A gazelle. A history. What is the difference?

By faith I am saved. By faith. That's what they say Peter preaches. But salvation is also by works. That's what I want. When I sew, the power of God is undeniable. I feel my thoughts as I sit in the dark. I have purpose. I have something to do.

Before Christ, I had a ship with only the idea of an ocean. After Christ, sewing is the ocean for me.

I light a torch and walk toward Simon's house, feeling my way along the street, hearing voices from within the houses I pass. In the meeting, they say another apostle, Luke, travels with Peter. In Samaria and Lydda, Luke was also with Jesus, writing about him. I think the disciples have been scattered all over the world. They are dispersed, running from persecution.

When Jesus wanted to wash Peter's feet, Peter asked to be washed all over. I laugh under my breath when I hear this.

Before he died, Jesus told Peter to feed his sheep. That does not make me laugh. Am I a sheep? The daughter of a craftsman. The wife of a merchant. The granddaughter of a woman who talked to me of the ideas men thought.

Uprising of Goats

I think of the sewing while the men talk. Yes, the sewing: embroidery, brocade, quilted work. The tunics, girdles, belts, sashes, cloaks, shawls, mantles. So many worn-out tunics and ragged garments in the marketplace. The children with nothing.

Sewing is the formation of ideas, the thoughts hanging in the *chitones*, the *pepla*. I like the changes, the transfiguration of the cloth.

In the street, I hear the crazy woman pass. She's the one with the cowlick in the front of her hair that makes the hair fall over her face.

Maybe she is speaking in tongues.

In Jerusalem, they crucified Jesus on a cross. Then we heard God raised him from the dead on the third day, and he showed himself openly.

I take stitches as I think of our blessings. The olive trees. The orchards. The risen Christ. The catacombs that hide the believers. I sew what I see with what I think. I sew garments from the cloth I buy at the wool and linen market. I buy needles too. Some I make from fishbone. I oil my thread.

Clothes are a resurrection.

I try to hold the Christians together with my sewing. I imagine them running. I build prisons for their persecutors with my needle. I stab the persecutors to death with the stitches I take. Then I hear about the conversion of one of the persecutors, the one who was named Saul. He is struck by a light on the road to Damascus. He is blinded, and Barnabas leads him into the city by the hand to Ananias, who prays for him. Saul's sight is restored. His name is changed to Paul, and he who once persecuted now preaches Jesus as the Son of God. I separate him with my needle. Saul is now a Christian. I know it happens because of the power in the threads.

We are called saints. *Hagioi*. Sanctified by the atoning blood of Christ. But what is atonement? What does it mean to be filled with the Holy Ghost? And what is a soul?

Are we the cloth draped to fit God? Or is he the idea of cloth draped to fit us?

I pray in my thoughts. My words are in the stitches I take with my needle.

One of the widows who had been sick dies. I see how thin she was as we wash her body.

"We don't live by bread alone," one of the women says. I hear the bitterness in her voice.

We wrap the woman's body with grave clothes, winding her feet together and covering her face. She looks like a fish that would feed the *ekklesia*[2] at Joppa. I embroider a pattern to close the graveclothes with my fishbone needle.

We hear from Jerusalem that the disciples pray and minister the word. Now the Greeks complain that the disciples neglect the widows. But the disciples can't leave the word of God and serve tables. They call us "widows" who lodge strangers, wash the saints' feet, relieve the afflicted, lived as wife to one husband, and are loved by our children. They look at us as though we are pigeons.

At my door, I pour water on the women's feet when they come to sew. "Wipe them on the mat," I say.

The girl wipes her feet twice.

Then we hear the Jews are incensed that Saul in now Paul. He persecuted the Christians. Now he is one of them? We know he was present at the stoning of believers. Now Paul knows what it is to run for his life.

One of the women smiles as she listens to the others talk.

I let the girl watch as I sew.

The disciples have to let Paul down over the wall in the basket. He escapes from Damascus and returns to Jerusalem. But in Jerusalem, the Christians are afraid of Paul. They won't believe he is a disciple filled with the Holy Spirit.

The woman talks as she sews. Her threads are artless. The girl sees me watching the woman's needle and she watches too. I nudge the girl's attention back to my sewing. The woman keeps talking. She says that in Jerusalem, Paul gets into trouble again. Now it's the Greeks who want to kill him. But Paul escapes to Caesarea and then Tarsus. Everyone hears about him in the churches in Judea and Galilee and Samaria.

Somehow, the churches keep growing.

Being a Christian is like being threaded through the shuttle that weaves the cloth. I think being filled with the Holy Ghost must be like having your mouth stuffed with threads that you try to spit out.

Down in the street there is a commotion. A donkey brays. Maybe he is tethered in the white heat of the sun.

2. "Church."

Uprising of Goats

My name means "gazelle." The gazelle runs and leaps. I think of this as I sit by the window and sew. Coats and garments, tunics and cloaks. I sew for the widows. Maybe it is foolish. I love to make clothes—shaping out of shapelessness the cloth that resists. It has to be cut. The cloth has to be sewed. It has to be shaped and held in place by cords and belts. At first, cloth is as unruly as the heart.

What do I understand by sewing? I try to tell them. I am sailing in the cloth. At night I feel the threads around me. That's the way I see heaven: a shaping of the shapeless.

My needle is a gazelle in the linen. How lovely and simple the sameness of each day, unless difference is in the clothes I make.

Simon, the tanner, works with his sandals. His house is on the sea. Does anyone question him?

The plainness of the sea has a beauty of its own. I sound like the Stoics I hear in the marketplace. I make a likeness of the sea with my cloth. "Forgive me," I say, "for loving the cloth, the little threads. I make the garments for others, but it's my own pleasure I get."

I feel the pain more often now.

I think about my husband, my father, and my grandmother. Sometimes I think they are waiting for me in a corner of the room, by my little table and vial of water. When no one is listening, I tell them to leave. Sometimes I poke them away with my needle. Sometimes I think of Hannah in the Scriptures, who sewed coats for her son, Samuel. Sometimes I let the girl thread my needle.

Somehow, the food I eat tastes different. I cannot swallow lamb any longer. What will it be like if I die? I hold my tunic closed as I stand on the roof of my house and look across the Mediterranean. I think of Jesus.

The Christians in Joppa don't have to meet in the catacombs. The meetings of our *ekklesia* take place in various houses since the *euangelista* came. The men read from the Scriptures for hours. For days. They discuss the prophecies while the women listen. They talk about speaking in tongues. Then we take communion and praise our God. Sometimes I feel my fingers move.

"Pentecost." What a word. *Pentekostos*, the fiftieth day after Passover. Think of them buzzing with other languages in an upper room. Think of the tongues of fire over their heads. I could embroider them on the *pepla*. Were they a mirage?

We heard that Peter spoke to those who thought the Christians were drunk. He quoted Joel, the Old Testament prophet, who prophesied God's spirit would be poured out. This *speaking in tongues* was what Joel meant.

How can Peter speak? The one who denied Christ three times. Maybe God overlooked his weakness. Maybe Peter forgave himself. Does he hear the roosters when they crow? Do they remind him? Is that why he is strong? Because he has so much weakness behind him? Do we live to blunder on? I think God keeps making cloth to cover us.

I let the girl have a needle. She holds it like a wiggling fish, or an eel in a basket, or the worms that come in with the ships.

It was the women who were at the tomb of Jesus first. The little sewing club. They were the ones to tell the men. But it was the men, the *euangelista*, who carried the news on the road from Jerusalem to all of us that Jesus was not in his tomb.

We also heard that some of the Christians were selling their possessions. We heard how the church grew daily.

I know I would not sell my possessions. I would not give my things away. My needles and threads. My bolts of cloth.

The women recount what they've heard of Peter as we sew. Peter must always be talking. I hear the women say they wish Peter would come to Joppa.

You can imagine how the Christians upset everyone. No wonder the believers are persecuted. They want to overturn the old ways with something that goes against understanding: a death on the cross, a resurrection from the tomb. By faith, we have died with Jesus and are born again. Our self-will is covered with the blood of Jesus. We are now two made one. Our self and Jesus, who is stronger. So we can draw on him. So we can be made whole in him. Until it seems that we are only him.

Even the believers have difficulty explaining.

The unbelievers ridicule us. I hear them as I buy figs and dates in the market. They are angry with the Christians. They don't like what the men say. They turn away, murmuring.

How many arguments are there? The believers and the unbelievers. The believers among themselves. The unbelievers among themselves. The Pharisees, with their talk of angels and resurrection. The Sadducees, who don't believe in either. The Stoics, who are fish caught in a net. Who stay there. The Epicureans, sorting for their pleasures. The Zealots, ripping out the threads that hold our world.

Joppa is a crossroads for the camel trains and trading ships. It is suspended between land and the sea. I hear talk of ideas from many places. They blur together like my own heritages.

The travelers also say that Peter has healed a lame man in Jerusalem. The elders and priests and scribes ask him by what power the lame man walks. Peter tells them, "It is Jesus, whom they crucified, whom God raised from the dead, even by him does this man stand here before you whole."

The stone that was called unimportant by the builders is become the head of the corner.

"Don't worry about Christianity," Gamaliel says to the unbelievers. If it isn't true, it comes to nothing (Acts 5:38).

Joppa is a seaport town. Have I said that? Situated on the Great Sea, the Mediterranean. Little Joppa with its cargo of good works sent out to the world.

Jerusalem is nearly a day's journey on a donkey. I have never been anywhere but Joppa. The ships must look at me strangely when they come to the shore. They must be like camels passing a tree that has to stand in one place.

My name is both languages. Dorcas is Greek. Tabitha, Hebrew.

I could have run a shipyard. I could have been a merchant. But I sew. It is the only voyage I have. I own my house. I am the captain of my own place, yet I am alone. I sit all day and sew. Sometimes my legs tremble when I stand. Sewing has its costs. The pain holds my body with its rope. I think I run like a gazelle toward death. Sometimes I feel my house has sails; I feel I am on the sea. I only have to look out my window to see the waves. Sometimes when I climb the stairs to the roof, I say I am standing on the ship's deck.

The pain is worse. I cannot eat figs any longer. They feel like donkey hooves in my mouth.

There is healing in Christ. I open my mouth. I try to speak in tongues. I hold up my hands. His words are my fish and bread.

Are tongues not a gift the Holy Spirit gives to his believers? If they are good little donkeys. If they carry the burdens they should.

Dorcas' Life

In the meeting of our *ekklesia*, I hear one of the men read from Neh 9:21: "Forty years God sustained them in the wilderness. They lacked nothing. Their clothes did not get old."

"Their clothes did not get old?" I ask suddenly, laughing. "Their clothes didn't wear out? What kind of threads made them? Did some angel mend the robes as the people slept? Did God breathe upon the cloth at night? How could cloth not wear out? Just look at the ragged children in the marketplace."

The people look at me. Why don't they say something?

"Cloth wears out," I say.

What did their clothes look like? The skin and bones of them. The texture and movement. How did the robes change from day to day? How could sameness work in cloth? Clothes are supposed to change, age, die. What if they didn't? How did the robes feel? Were the people aware that their clothes didn't wear out? Something that didn't change didn't belong to the person who changed as they wore it. I ask them in the meeting, "Why am I the only one who thinks of this?"

Sometimes I can only work a few hours. My body throbs the way my foot does. I think my foot is now my whole body.

I walk to the market for herbs and lentils. I walk on my camel foot.

I want to push the crowds out of my way. The goats and rams. The little crates of chickens. The rooster. Pigeons. The noise of them all. The juggler tries to get my attention. I push past him with my basket.

Maybe I'll walk across the water; they say Jesus did. I want to walk across the sea to the far places where the merchants come from. Sometimes I hold to the side of the houses when I return from the market.

Simon, the tanner, carries my basket of fish. Does he think I'll ask him to share it with me?

I hear the language of others on the street. It must be like tongues in the upper room. Everyone speaking their own language; no one understanding, but I know it is serviceable. I know it is language. Not a voice wasted. I do not think the Holy Spirit visits me with tongues.

Who is the Holy Spirit? A *folios*[3] who watches a sepulcher? A shadow who won't let me pass?

My voice is in my threads. Sometimes I hear them speak. I think the sound of my sewing has the power of a tongue. I feel the needle in my hand.

3. "Guard."

My hands tremble as I work. I see the women watch my hands. I wonder if they hear my threads.

"I will help you with the needle," the girl says.

"You can't even hold your own needle the way I say," I tell her. "How can you help me?"

She sits beside me on the little footstool, watching her feet when I am angry with her.

Why am I angry?

The threads chap my hands. I rub oil on my fingers. They smell like flax. They are rough as the dried nets of fishermen.

I want to walk the dusty streets of Joppa, but my feet won't walk.

In the night, I think the sea is dry. The ships have wheels like a cart. They are pulled by donkeys and camels.

I think of Noah, or John the Baptist wearing skins, with his hive of bees.

I can't stand on the roof at night and look across the sea. But I know there is something moving over the world. All worldly. I feel a pain sharp as scissors. My mattress is wet with sweat. I shiver in the night breeze. I can't lean down to pull up my covers.

A needle is the rage of heaven. To sew keeps the fish away. The conspiracy of fish. The fish have legs that open from their side when they come to shore. They walk through Joppa at night. Sometimes they step into the sky.

When the women come to sew, I ask them to move my bed so I can see the sky. I don't tell them the stars are fish in the dark. I don't tell the women how the fish scales glisten in the room. The fish are taking over. They are jugglers in the marketplace. The fish sweat as they try to get their breath.

I dream of a foot with eyes and ears. The women's voices have edges like a sparrow's chirp.

I hear the crazy woman in the street. I think she speaks in a trance.

The women have threads hanging from their eyes when they come to my house. They have fishermen's floats for ears. Sometimes I cannot even sit up in bed. The women prop me against a sack of cloth. I grip the edge of my mattress. My breath won't come.

I feel the scissors again. Someone is cutting me out of my body.

Then there's another pain. Unlike the others. Maybe it's the girl trying to stitch me with her crazed needle.

I see the walls of my room transfigured as cloth. They move closer when they don't think I'm looking.

The sky has a moon and a sun for eyes.

Dorcas' Life

There is a bleeding hand above my bed. It must have been poked with a needle. The blood drops on my head.

How much fabric of days and nights?

The women sew in my house. They swim through my room like fish. They nibble my arms. I try to hold my arms away. They hold my arms down so they can eat.

Is that my own voice I hear? It sounds like someone howling.

The moon is a leper's hand without fingers. The moon is the palm of a hand. The shape of the moon is a hand of another shape.

What is that clanging?

Water is squeezed into my mouth from a cloth. Once I choke.

The moon is stabbed. Blood drips from it.

Death is facing the self by itself. The women are with me. But it is myself I sit by. The hard little knot of the self.

My lungs suck for air.

The sun turns cold and goes out with everything in it.

A Chapter in Which an Afterword to Dorcas and a Divorce Begins

The wild goat will call to his fellow.

—Isa 34:14

I CONTINUED WITH DORCAS, ca. 40 AD.

Did I actually believe Dorcas was speaking to me? Did I think these voices were making the rounds, so to speak, looking for someone who would listen? Was I the chosen?

I always noticed the goats grazing on trips through Texas, their noses to their work.

My tenure review was on my mind. I had struggled with publications. A few articles here and there. I had edited an anthology that received favorable reviews. I had a book in progress with the working title, *Biblical Texts, Christian Narratives*, with a focus on the way the shape of the text influenced the narrative. It would be an accumulation of my lectures. That was another reason I wrote them out so carefully.

On a particularly sour afternoon, I was given more advisees. A colleague received a fellowship I had also applied for, and I had to be congratulatory. The chair of the department asked me to attend a meeting he didn't want to attend. I had to visit a lawyer's office to go over the divorce agreement. Walker was not going to refute it. It seemed we had come to

A Chapter in Which an Afterword to Dorcas and a Divorce Begins

an agreeable end to our marriage. It was like an old piece of clothing I no longer wanted to wear.

I sat in church on Sunday asking for a sign. Or was I crazy with injustice? Natting like a goat in class until they led me to another pasture where I could eat stones? I prayed for my decision to divorce. Was it wrong? Yes it was, in part. But I was going to do it. I prayed for my own work. Was it wrong? Building onto a structure already in place? A holy place at that, which I considered Scripture to be. Was I building what amounted to a shed, a lean-to added onto a cathedral? Forgive me, but these words speak. I am overrun with voices. They are already overspread.

Once in a while, I found pleasure in teaching. To stand in front of a class that had read the assignment and understood, before students who had opinions, arguments, thoughts to share. What a pleasure to start a discussion, to hear the students continue on their own, to stand back, to hear them augment the text with their own interpretations. To guide sometimes, to suggest, to remind them of the trail. Underneath that pleasure was the pleasure of returning to my office to find the thread of Dorcas' voice. Especially when the students quoted my colleague, Justine Crowd, the religion department's atheist. Maybe then I watched the clock that would eventually cut them off.

Then I felt the same voice coming. *Leave me—oh, don't leave me.*

II

Dorcas' Death

Each of us finds the world of death fitted to himself.

—Virgil, *The Aeneid*

Dying is not a dry sea. It is walking into water. I don't want to get wet. I don't want to be with those who swim and move their gills. Their large eyes. But these aren't fish here; these are old beings who walk with me. They are kissing my legs. *Get away.* I poke them with my needle until they are full of holes.

    I try to speak, but the soggy shore sinks under my feet. I am going somewhere, but I don't like it. I must think to keep my head. I must remember, must imagine. My needle swings in the cloth. My needle follows Christ. My needle is Christ.

    There is a sense of floating, the way fish move one way and then the other in the water. There is the needle of a boat bobbing through the cloth. I take faith from my needle. A needle is a stem from which heaven grows. It is a core, a kernel. It has the smell of the sea. I cannot let it go. I cannot let myself be pulled away. What is happening? My thoughts are waves running everywhere without a needle stitching them.

    The nostrils of the camel widen when they smell the sharp water. A needle draws throats together.

Dorcas' Death

You can cut your foot against the sea. Whole continents overlap the ocean. The thoughts of heaven spill like waves to the shore. I think of a fisherman's float. Nets of fishes. Their eyes embroidered by a needle. The angels sew the scales on the fish. They sweat in the heat. A smaller angel wipes their foreheads. Heaven is full of perrons.

"It is he who builds his stories in the heavens" (Amos 9:6). Heaven is full of thoughts. Just as I wanted it to be. One thought follows another without pausing. I fly on the winds of thought.

The camels turn back toward the desert, where they want to go.

The sandstorms are needles traveling to Joppa from the desert.

I think of them on the shore of heaven.

Quiet. Listen to the needles. They talk, but they don't think I hear them. Sometimes I hear them speak in tongues. I don't understand their words, but I hear them. The needle is a wound. It heals by faith. It is a ship that travels where I can't. It is a flock of sheep. A harbor from the sea.

In heaven there is a family of needles: Grandmother. Father. Husband. Children.

The church of needles sticks in the folds of the ocean. There is drying in the needles. They walk to the shore.

I put my hands to my head to feel my thoughts.

The trees are needles in heaven.

I say, "Up there somewhere—Jerusalem—the New Jerusalem."

I learn that I have to learn Scriptures to get into heaven. I see there is something I can't see beyond. I see the dead memorizing the words: "The pastures are clothed with flocks" (Ps 65:13).

I say my own Scriptures: "He clothes the sea with waves."

God does not like it. I have to get back in line with everything I learned.

There is drying in the Scriptures.

I think in Joppa the women are washing me and draping me in cloth. I can't feel their cloths sneaking my arms, but I think they are. Maybe the girl is standing with them.

I want to be with Christ and his saints, all sewing. Even Christ embroiders. Sometimes I see beyond the fog. I see heaven's storeys are full of thread. I see circles of needles in heaven. I have never seen such spirals, such patterns. I could never imagine them. No. Storey upon storey. Place upon place. Heaven upon heaven.

Uprising of Goats

Beyond the Scriptures, I see there are closets in heaven. Full of shawls and mantles. Tunics with sashes and belts. I see the tunics becoming ephods. They are also tied with sashes, but held at the shoulders with shining ornaments like little moons. I see the transformation of cloth. The resurrection of sewing. Plain shawls and tunics become priests' coats and robes, ephods and breastplates, girdles and mitres.

Maybe the river of heaven is for washing the clothes.

I want to say, I am the Bride of Christ. I am the Bride of Heaven. I am the Bride of New Jerusalem.

My husband is here. We are spirits meeting one another with reserved joy. I can't say that I see him clearly; he is in a fog. I would think we were in Joppa on one of those evenings when the fog crowds in from the sea and the stars don't flicker. I speak briefly, but after that I can't think of what to say.

It is my grandmother's thoughts I hear. But when I turn to her, she has moved on. I want to sew threads that look like her voice when it left her mouth.

I look for my father.

What else is up here?

Who else is up here?

This is death?

I will say I am a widow doing what needed to be done. I will say when we met for water at the well, I could see the worn folds in their garments. I wanted to sew for them. I wanted to clothe them. I watched them walk from the well with their heavy earthen water-jars. I thought only of them.

I am still in line. There are people ahead of me with their arms missing; parts of their bodies bitten away.

But which line am I in? Do we stand in the same line only to be separated? I look for someone I know. I look for someone to tell me.

God is trying to take the needle from my hand. I will not let go. I can't get along without it. I want to embroider the circles of heaven. *The layers of the heavenlies.* The flying clothes.

"Stop it!" I say to God. I jerk the needle away from him. The needle is myself.

I want to step onto the ridges of heaven. I think they are thoughts.

There are closets that move outward in a coil. Blessed needles. Holy ephods and mitres. I am coming.

Dorcas' Death

Tabitha.

I look to see who addresses me by my other name. Who is it? Someone I don't know. Surely.

Death is a relief from suffering.

There is goodness. I could last. As long as there are needles and thread. Some of the women were in their pleated *chitones*.

I see God and his brooches. The main fullness at the front and back, not bunched at the sides. It is not simple to drape the tunics, the shorter *himatioi* with scallops.

Sometimes I walk by the sea to feel the scallops on the shore under my feet. The sea is a moving garment. A living garment.

I have another Scripture verse to learn. What good does praying do now?

There are seams of thought after the world. I stand on the selvedge.

It is like the nights that are full of the moon, and I stand on the roof of my house and look at the sea. I know what the sea looks like during the day, but in the darkness, I can only see the shadows of it.

That's where I stand, on the shore of heaven. Trying to look ahead.

But I don't go forward yet. I know what's there. But it does not yet have words.

Someone keeps calling me, pulling me back.

I drive him away with the sword of my needle, but I hear his voice again: *Tabitha.*

There are stories that return the dead. Elisha called a child back to life (2 Kgs 4:33–35). Jesus called a girl (Matt 9:18). The Apostle Paul brought Eutychus back to life after he fell out of a third-story window, having fallen asleep while Paul was preaching (Acts 20:12). Everyone will be raised (1 Cor 15:52).

We have the Scriptures. We heard Christ's words. We heard what was happening in Jerusalem from those who passed through Joppa.

How much this place is like those words.

Beyond the closets, I see a vast city of people. Streets. A river. Somewhere, a throne. I see heaven is full of flying beings. Birds. Crowned pigeons. Their eyes red as heaven, their breasts blue as the sky and sea kissing at dusk. Their headdresses topped with white-tipped feathers. They have constellations on their heads. There are "granges." Words I don't know. Palm trees in oasis after oasis. Landscapes of mountains and desert. The elements are in heaven—wind, the draperies of light. Creatures I have never seen wearing tunics with slits from which light sneezes. Animal beings wearing something like fish scales, something sewn as if it took words to tell. Others have feathers like vents of the smallest windows. And there are the noises. The singings. Winged gazelles with spots and stripes.

There's a hierarchy in heaven.

Closets full of garments I have sewn. I cannot explain.

I wish I had used more than one thread on a needle. Threads of different colors. Why didn't I know? Maybe if I had prayed. Maybe if I had tongues. Why didn't God make it clear? I feel my anger. I want to rework all I have sewn. I see the garments differently now; I see them as garments within garments.

Everything seems sudden. As if forming. The cloth cut but not yet sewn.

What is happening? Everything changes. I feel I am falling. My house, the ship, is sinking. What do they do at sea when their ship is going down?

Those women in my house. Is one of them helping the girl sew?

Back into the soppy water.

Peter is praying to Jesus. Peter is asking him to call me back.

Calling me to this word, this call, *this*.

I feel the tenderness of the cloth over my body. The group of women. They cry and I want to tell them not to cry. Then Peter comes and they plead with him. I am far away when I hear him say—it is simple: *Tabitha*. I open my eyes and see the disciple. I know he is Peter. The power of his word pulls me. I am on the shore of heaven when I hear his voice. I am stepping into the circles of heaven that last forever. I am a captain of the sea of needles. And Peter calls me back! I can't move my feet. They are held together with fins, as a fish's. I see the starfish in the water. I see they are my hands. I have become the sea.

Heaven is a garment I wear. The lovely folds of cloth flowing.

But a voice calls me back. It has been done before. Don't I know?

I feel my feet caught in a fish net. I am not finished with seeing yet.

Thruck. I feel the gauze of the world is mesh. The nets *enmesh*.

There are spaces somewhere between the seas in heaven, and a voice that calls me back.

A Chapter in Which an Afterword to Dorcas Continues

It was the best class. It was the worst.

I only wanted to return to my office to work.

Often I looked at my watch.

Often I made a note of something I wanted to include in the proposal.

I WAS WRITING THE voices of biblical women. There were faculty meetings in which we shared our research. I meant to talk about my work-in-progress, *Biblical Texts, Christian Narratives*, but I got into the voices. I didn't mean to talk about them. I wanted to keep them private—my own place, a garden in the back of a house that could not be seen from the street. The other faculty looked at me as I spoke in the meeting. I tried to cut off my remarks, but there were questions. Maybe scoffing. Was this a form of nonfiction? What theories did I tie my work to? What grounding? Was it creative writing? What genre? Was it acceptable scholarship?

That evening, I read about Samson, who killed a lion and later found honey in the carcass (Judg 14). The voices of the biblical women were the honey I found in my struggle with teaching. Samson's mother's voice came to me momentarily. Wasn't she nameless? An angel had announced Samson's birth to her. Then she watched him marry Philistine women. Eventually blinded, he pulled down the columns of a structure, killing three thousand Philistines, as had been promised—just not in the way she expected. I could hear her grief, as I could the mother of Sisera, who watched from the window for the return of his chariot after he had been killed by Jael, a woman

(Judg 5:28). *Why is his chariot so long in coming?* She answered herself: *Have they not divided the spoil? To every man a damsel or two, to Sisera a spoil of dyed garments with needlework suitable for the necks of those who take the spoil?*

I shut myself away for the weekend. I had to finish my letter for tenure. It was more than a letter. I would have to come up with pages—eleven single-spaced pages once it was finally finished—detailing the history of my education, the subjects I taught, my course development, publications, scholarship, committees, conferences, fellowships, and recognition, if any, in my field. All the while, the voices pulled me: Caleb said that whoever smites Kiriath-sepher would be given Achsah, his daughter, in marriage (Josh 15:16). Othniel, Caleb's nephew, took Kiriath-sepher, and Caleb gave Achsah to him. She went to her father Caleb and said, "You have given me the south land. Now give me also the springs of water." And he gave her the springs.

Achsah had no choice in marriage. Maybe she liked Othniel. Maybe he was the one she wanted. Maybe not. The Scripture does not say. But what it does say is that she asked for her part. I kept Achsah in mind as I worked on my case for tenure, writing and rewriting the letter. Reading and rereading it. Trembling, sometimes, as I wrote—as I prepared the three required notebooks: my scholarship, my committee work and conference participation, and my teaching evaluations, most of which were positive. Though I'd been called to the department head's office, I had students grateful for my classes.

The department head signed my letter requesting tenure. The department members wrote their own letters, which I could later see, if I desired. They had colleagues in other departments write letters of support. There were outside reviewers, some of which I recommended, while others were unknown to me. They would read my files and write their estimation of my qualifications.

I felt an opening of my life. A passage into another part separate from the earlier part. Homework now had another meaning. It was a term I could interpret in another way.

The girls left for college before I knew it. Walker drove us there. I was grateful that he came to help us move in. I didn't long for him. I didn't want him to return. It had been a long time coming. I had kept house and raised the

A Chapter in Which an Afterword to Dorcas Continues

girls. I was grateful that I didn't have to work during those early years, but could instead stay home and continue my education, which had been cut off by marriage and the birth of children. I had taken care of all the details. Maybe it was my fault that I felt alone. I never asked Walker to help. He mowed the lawn but hired help for everything else. I folded the laundry, shopped for the groceries, cooked all the meals. I cleaned the house and kept track of everyone. Reminding them of appointments. Taking them where they needed to go. I was aware of something inside. A distance. There were other reasons than the fire. The fire was the finality. It represented the burning of the past. I had raised two daughters. I had finished my education with a PhD in religious studies. My dissertation was published by an academic press.

I had waited a long time. At one of our counseling sessions, the pastor told me I was selfish. Yes, I suppose that was it. It was my turn to do what I wanted. I had not wanted to continue with Walker. We had had a long marriage. But I wanted to be away from it also.

I had applied to teach at a college and was accepted. I had felt a yearning. No, it was a definite place within me. I had something to do. I had a presence about me.

I remembered the interview. No, I had not taught anywhere. I had just received my PhD. I taught the girls' Sunday school classes. I was the soccer coach one year until another mother took the job. Girl Scouts. What made me think I could teach on a college level? Well, I had a sense that something was before me. An interest in biblical language. Its meaning. It was something I had waited a long time to take part in. In the beginning, the college hired me as a lecturer. Now I was associate professor up for tenure. Maybe it was selfish, but it was what I decide to be.

III

Peter Calls Dorcas Back

Like a broken tooth and a foot out of joint.

—Prov 25:19

Why would I come back to life?

To hear the leper's bell? To be followed by the crazy woman? To watch the waves of her hair? To see the lame? Blind? Deaf? To live without the circles of heaven I saw? Why would I want to return to this ugliness? Ugliness. In this life, I am not a gazelle, but a goat.

Peter has my hand; I draw it back. I want to snip off his arm, but I remember I must be polite.

There's something strange in my room. Strange. What am I doing here?

"She's alive," Peter says and looks at me like he hardly believes it himself.

I don't seem any different. I don't know what to say. What does he want? We are standing in my room, but I can't take a step because the grave clothes are bound at my feet.

The room is stark. Ugly.

I am hungry for heaven.

Peter calls the women into my room. They stand gawking at me. No one knows what to say. They are amazed I am alive.

Peter Calls Dorcas Back

Peter leaves the room.

One of the women helps me to sit on the bed. They undo the grave clothes. The girl stands at my side.

"I am thirsty," I say. The girl brings my pitcher of water.

Someone hands me the tunic they left on a peg, but it is soiled. They didn't have time to wash it, they say.

I ask for the women to leave me alone. I feel to see whether my hair is tied back like it always is. One woman stays to bring me a clean tunic. I ask the girl to leave.

Downstairs, I hear them talking to Peter. The woman helps me dress, then leaves the room too. I sit on the bed. I want to cry, but I will not let the tears run down my face. We don't always get to do what we want, I tell myself. But I am angry. The first time I was ever going someplace, I was returned to Joppa.

I am bothered by the ugliness for a few days. I can't tell them what I see, but there are lovely clouds over Joppa, like the underside of heaven. And there are ships spinning on the ocean—and sewing, yes, sewing.

At first, the world does not seem to fit. But I sew the city. Whole worlds in my hands.

They look at me when I walk to the fish market on the shore: the women with their bundles and palm-frond baskets. I do not like it. I see the juggler and the traveling players with their puppets. My lungs fill and I want to cry out for the world, for the lost and suffering people, but I sweep the feelings back. The Holy God loves his minnows. He gives us Jesus, the minnow basket. Jesus, the minnow lover.

Will I feel pain again? Will I have strength to sew? How will I die again?

The stars are lanterns in the heavens. The flames waver in the evening breeze from the sea. Someone is stitching by the light of her lamp. I can follow the pattern like birds in the open air.

At night, I lift my hand to the sky as though God will pull me back.

I have fits of hunger for heaven. For the vast coils that move outward. I see them in the spirals of a tiny shell. I open my mouth and bite the air.

I see we are what we make ourselves to be—in Christ, of course. The heaven I saw was his: his open rooms, his closets full of enormity.

Uprising of Goats

Now I walk through the markets in Joppa. Over there, I see Peter by the stalls and booths.

Do I feel the wind from the sea? Was I sucked through the water on my way back? Yes, we get to the earth through the sea. Isn't the birth of a child the arrival of a fish?

The girl follows me through the booths at the market, past the braying animals, the tethered bullock. She stumbles on my tunic as she watches the players with their puppets. She wants me to make a puppet for her.

I watch the players move the puppets. Is that the way Christ works with us?

"Look here," I tell her. The flour of wheat, barley, spelt, millet; the olive oil from the stone presses; the beans and lentils; the raisins, figs, dates, apricots, pomegranates, apples, mulberries, melons, and lemons; the cucumbers, onions, leeks, garlic, and endive. The salt, cinnamon, rue, dill, cumin, coriander, capers, saffron, and mustard. The lamb, fish, beef, doves, sparrows. I go over them as if they were the stitches I take in my cloth.

Now the girl watches the woman with the grasshoppers. She watches her remove the head, the feet, the wings, the entrails. She watches her set aside the other grasshoppers that have dried. She crushes them into a cake and cooks them in water with salt or fries them in oil and serves them with honey.

I think about Hannah in heaven. I wonder if she still sews little coats for her son, Samuel. Maybe in heaven (if I had stayed there) we could sew together at her house.

What is a soul? Maybe it is a fish that lives in the sea that is heaven, which is somewhere in my head when I die, when I am clothed with the sea, when I have what I learned on earth.

Hannah took Samuel to Shiloh and left him with the priest. How hard that must have been. But we all lose our children one way or another, though Hannah later had other children.

When I walk to the market, I always see Peter. I try to be grateful, feeling awkward with him beaming over me. I was dead and now I live. He touches my shoulder, and I want to withdraw. I don't like going to the market. I don't like everyone looking at me.

Peter Calls Dorcas Back

Sometimes I look for the flying beings I saw in heaven. The ones with red eyes. Sometimes I sew several threads together. The way I remember. How can I make the sewing look like what I saw?

Sometimes when I look up from sewing, the women look away from me quickly.

I blot the tea I spill when I rise quickly to get the door. I'm not used to company. I'm used to being by myself, except for the women who sew. I abide them, but I feel frightened at the arrival of the others. I stand at my door and look. Then they are in my house asking questions. They don't sew, but they want to know what was it like—what I remember of death.

"Do we remember our sins?" they ask in *ekklesia*. "What is it like to see heaven?"

I say, "In heaven I should try not to sew. But I cannot stay away. The needle jumps into my hand. The voice is a needle sewing." What have I forgotten? I say, "I think we recite Scriptures in heaven, or just before there." They have to walk into the sea, I tell them. "Not the shore of Joppa. No. There's another shore. Somewhere."

"But where?" they ask.

I try to sew. But they keep asking. I was there. How can I not talk of it? I run into a storm in my sewing as I talk.

"Heaven, or the edge of it, which is all I saw," I tell them, "is a crowd on the shore when the fishing boats come in. Everyone hurrying for the fish."

There is confusion. Shoving. Irritation. I think now that none of it was clear. Heaven hides itself. Heaven is clothed. Heaven is closets. Full of marketplaces with a multitude of happenings. Clefts in the rock. I am not making sense. Weren't there even stalls and closets and storeys in the ark?

I see they are disappointed in what I can tell them.

In the Scriptures, there are what seem to be sewing lessons. I think sometimes I want to teach. I want to tell the girl that Hannah's little boy, Samuel, wore coats she made for him. She took them when she went with her husband from Ramathaim-zophim to Shiloh to offer the yearly sacrifice.

When Samuel became a priest, he was clothed in a linen ephod, which is something I tell her she couldn't do, not being a priest, at least while she's in this life.

I tell the women that God cares for sewing. His instructions for the ephod and the holy clothes are in Exod 28.

Uprising of Goats

I think I will make ephods, which are tunics before their transformation. I think of cutting the hole for the neck and sewing the woven work around it. My ephods would fly around the room like birds.

The words about sewing lift themselves up from the Scriptures. They make their way into my head, onto the shore of my thoughts, into the determination of my will. I think we live to sew.

I am always high with Scriptures. Why? I am still learning verses.

Time is an emptiness. What will I do if I don't sew? I have to have purpose. I have to know what to do. The words about sewing speak to me.

I can't pass a day without knowing I will accomplish something with my efforts. I watch the path of my needle through the cloth. I can forget time; it is timeless, because of the loveliness of sewing.

I wait for another morning in my bed. Sometimes I think I can work by my lamp through the night, but my eyes sting. Sometimes the needle fuzzes as it goes into the cloth. I want to say, "fuzzle." I decide to turn out my lamp. Lord God of hosts, keep my eyesight. Keep my ships in the night. May I not have been brought back to be blind.

If only linen would hold dye, I would use the purple from sea mollusks and the *tekhelet*.

The girl does not come. We hear from a neighbor that there is a disabled ship trying to enter the bay. We leave our sewing.

The *artemon*[1] sticks up like a cross from the water. I see Peter praying. The sailors will not be able to bring the ship into the harbor. Several boats row toward it. The oars are the wings of small insects. We hear the sailors yell as the ship sinks. The divers cannot retrieve the cargo—any of it. The rescue boats are loaded with men as they return. The captain paces the shore while the fishing boat brings him in. He is trying to absorb what has happened. He is thinking of the cloth that is lost.

The choppy little waves, quick to touch the shore, are nervous sparrows. The larger waves come from the suck of the ship after it goes down. We step back when we see the waves coming.

The noise of the crowd is *spurted*. There are quick, abrupt voices. I must get a hold of the *klasma*.[2] Slow the voices before they shred into pieces. Behind them I hear the mourning doves.

1. "The foresail."
2. "Scraps."

Peter Calls Dorcas Back

I wake in the night to listen to the sailors in the street. They are drunk with the loss of their ship. They want to dive for the cargo. They argue whether it can be done. Leave it in the bottom of the ocean, I would say to them. What is lost doesn't come back. You can pick it up on your way to heaven.

The next morning, I tell the women how to weave their needle through the cloth. Where does their lack of ideas come from? I could not face my days without sewing. Some are just there to talk. The loneliness is deafening.

I put the girl's work on the bottom when she is gone. I don't want it touching mine or the others'. I want a separate place for it. I would like to say, "Let the needle rest in your lap. Let it loose a moment." I can hear her needle grieve over its path, over its lot, over having to go where it doesn't want to guided by someone who doesn't know how to guide, someone whose thoughts don't encompass it, who makes it do something it doesn't want. To do lesser than it is capable of when it has a vision of what it can do: that is its fate in the girl's hand. To go crooked and without satisfaction all its days. Plow, little needle in your field from which nothing grows.

She is *kophos*.[3]

Sometimes my needle gives me trouble. I get it back into line. "Do your duty," I tell it. "Above all, be wise."

Sometimes I want to beat the walls. I stomp my feet on the floor. I feel so enclosed in this life; I want to poke holes in myself.

Sometimes I think I remember being born. I remember being put in the garment of this body. I remember the tightness around me. I felt my feet sewn to the bottom of my skin. I would be in this small house all my life. No wonder I bucked like a donkey: I wanted to be loosed—the way I was before I was born. I think we long for it all our lives.

A woman gives money to the church and her husband is angry. I hear them in the next house. He starts to beat her. She runs from the house. He beats her in the street.

I take my needle, sew his fingers closed, sew his arms to his body.

What do I do when something I want to do is wrong as well as right?

If only he could see heaven.

I dream of cloth that will fit like the skin of a gazelle. Not like the coarse cloth we have. Even the wool has a will of its own. But this cloth I

---

3. "Dull."

saw in heaven is like skin itself, fitting what it comes next to. In heaven, God knows how.

I prick my finger. My blood is red. But I see blue in the standing veins in my old hands. How does it change? Like a fine silk fabric changes shades in the light and shadows? Like the ground under the olive tree? The sun and shade on the dirt road? The evening sky when I can withdraw into the house to eat my evening meal and sleep?

All the sky changes as it moves. I know the moon is the palm of a hand that bleeds.

What dreams roar in my head like the turning of the sea in a storm? Maybe it's the groundedness so close to the rocking sea. It is the cradle of a child I do not have. Or the grandchildren that keep other women busy.

The head is hard. Not like the heart. No, I won't cut the heart loose from the thread that holds it in the chest. But the head, the thinking; that's what I want. Just thinking the thread through the material, planning the cloak. How the embroidery will cross it like a camel.

Christians. *Christianos*. Those speaking-in-tongues ones. Those give-away-their-possessions ones. They say it that way. Christian. Belonging to Christ.

A fish is our symbol. Because we're going to the sea.

Jesus walked across the water. If I step into it, I would go down like the ship; I would drown. There is no hope of walking on the water for me. I don't think there is for them either.

The needle sinks into the cloth when I hold it there. Why would Jesus want to walk on water? Now I know it is to keep from sinking.

There are fish in the thinking.

They say Jesus did such things. He pulled a coin from a fish's mouth (Matt 17:27). I'm surprised everyone isn't looking into the mouth of every fish he pulls from the sea. But I see the coins here, in the waves that spill onto the shore like bags of silver coins. All the people at the fishmarket on the shore. The marks from high and low tide.

Where is common sense? Where is fish sense?

They would stay in the water if they could. The fish don't come on land looking for us.

Blue blood. Red blood. A difference that can't be explained, unless we are like the sky turning red and blue in the evening, unless the sky leaks out from inside us.

Why do we need Jesus? I think in the meeting of the *ekklesia*.

Jesus stirs up the road, even after his death. The dust doesn't settle once he's passed. He causes the people to argue. The women speak out. The men tell us to be quiet. We pray while Peter and the men talk about Scriptures. No one agrees. It brings out the worst in us, yet it causes thought.

I was sitting with my husband as he breathed his last breath. It seemed he just folded up like a marketplace at four in the afternoon. Everyone went home, and he was no more.

I saw my husband in heaven. I told him I remembered the cornerstone in our house, the ceremony when it was set. We didn't know what to say beyond that. I think about him and miss him. I think sometimes he would flop back, just as a fish tries to return to water before it dies. But I've died and now I live. What is the difference?

Sometimes in the night, heaven comes in the light of the moon. Heaven is there in the corner of the room. All of heaven? It only enlarges as you see it. How do I explain? Sometimes I stand on my roof and try to see the tunics flying to heaven.

"What should I do with this thread?" the woman asks.

"Snip it off with your teeth," I tell her. I see the cloth pucker when she sews. "Look here," I say, "think of the Lord while you sew. That will help the needle go straight into the cloth. You have to risk *unloading the ship*." I say one thing to her while thinking another.

The girl is sweeping threads, making mounds of them on the floor.

Jesus walked on the earth for a few years and was crucified. Now you find us scattered and ignorant of what was actually meant by it all. If you looked away once, just once, it was over.

What are we supposed to do? Join a group and live in the hills eating locusts and honey, wearing camel hair and badger skins? I wouldn't like that.

I hear Peter talking. He sees me coming before I can turn away. The people turn and look. Am I supposed to spill over in gratefulness? What does he expect? What do the people want to see?

Peter had to pray to Jesus. It was Jesus who pushed me back to Joppa.

I only want to get past them and go to the market. I want to buy flour and spices, raisins and melons. I only want to get back to my sewing. I listen to Peter talk. I go when I can.

Uprising of Goats

We are in *ekklesia* at Simon's house. The whole place smells like hide. I don't like to sit without a needle in my hand; I feel enclosed. I make long journeys across the cloth when I sew.

Peter says, "We are saved by faith."

What does he mean?

"Can I sit in my house and do nothing?" I ask.

Does he mean, *I can't trust my sewing*? As if it were not a ladder to heaven, as if it were not the wings I fly on. Or the ship I sail upon the sea.

The Christians look at me. There is argument over salvation: whether it is by faith or works. The small group is in an uproar. I sit on one of Simon's stools, quivering. What is it I feel? Rage?

When light is on the sea, I watch the needles sewing the water, holding it in place.

I hear Peter talking to the woman whose husband beat her. He tells her to stay with the man. I hear him on the street. Heaven is obedience to God. I do not think so. Who has been to heaven already? Is it him?

I think heaven is far out in the water. The little waves stop, and there is a hole, and we sink into it and become fish and are caught in the net and suffocate. Then we are scattered into another place.

I divide my days like God.

"The Lord God made coats of skins and clothed them" (Gen 3:21). Adam and Eve were dressed in blood. That's what was shed to get the animal skins.

I see Simon and his sandals made of hides. I still wear palm bark on my feet.

Simon in his apron, with his vat of salts for tanning. What does he talk about with Peter?

How can I remember what happened in heaven?

Sewing is the way, the truth, the life.

Now get busy; work. Weren't those the angel's words?

We are on earth in our skulls with ears and eyes. We wear our veils and head coverings, not knowing anything, not seeing with our stupid feelings, raging and leading the wrong way. No, it is the mind which is the compass, the guide and rudder that says, "Walk on, don't ask, don't know, just live by faith and work."

Heaven is always coming into the room. I think instead they should look into the sea.

Would Joppa float underwater? Would the camels and beavers and donkeys swim if the sea came upon us? Somehow we rise.

They ask me but I cannot say how.

I think the net of stars is our catch. I belong to the fishermen of the heavens. Not underwater.

What gracious God would leave us to rest under piles of water? He promises dry ground. Did not Israel cross?

"Dorcas," the child calls.

"What?"

"Can I come in?"

I don't answer.

"Who are you talking to?" she asks.

"What do you want?" I answer.

"Something to sew."

"You just want to make a mess. I'm busy. Go to the well and fill the jug with water. I want to wash my eyes. They hurt when I work. My eyes feel swollen bigger than a camel's. I think it's the dust from the street. Then you can recite to me. Something they teach you in church."

"But I want to sew."

"Get the water."

There is writing on tablets or parchments the priests can read, but the women have to listen to the priests, or to Peter, or to the teachers, who are men.

What should I do with my thoughts, which are always pushing in? I am so impatient. So abrupt. I try to calm myself. I feel my thoughts like garlic and leeks when I stand in the market and turn them in my hands. I can also turn my thoughts over with my threads.

I talk to the girl when she returns.

After the flood, in the Scriptures, when Noah and his family departed from the ark on Mount Ararat, Japhet, Noah's son, settled on a hill overlooking a bay. He called it *Yafo*, "lovely." Later, Joppa was a part of the allotment of Dan when the tribes of Israel entered the promised land. Joppa on the Plain of Sharon. A seaport of Jerusalem.

The girl has to listen if she wants to sew. I tell her, "They wrap our feet together when we die. We walk with what we know." It's why we live. To speak with our threads, our thoughts spilling waves hard as rocks.

"Have you received the Holy Spirit since you believed?" a woman asks as we sew.

"No, but I've received threads," I say.

She looks at me. The other women watch us.

"The threads flow through my fingers," I tell her. "They talk with their tongues."

When we are alone, I rub oil on my sore hands. I speak to the girl again.

The girl holds her fingers in her ears. I tell her to take her hands away or I will poke her hands with my needle.

I tell her our ears are holes opened with needles. Our hearing comes from suffering. The more we suffer, the more we hear.

The girl says I am mean as her mother. She cries, and I take away her needle. I tell her she must think and not cry.

My mother lived by her feelings. I do not want to remember her. I tell the girl if she is quiet, I will give back her needle. We must be quiet and not get in trouble.

I don't want to be a mother angry with her daughter, but the girl is irritating. God must understand. And forgive. The girl gets in the way. She is insistent. She reminds me of when I was a girl. I don't want to remember; I want to leave my anger. I continue talking to the girl about Joppa in the Scriptures. Joppa the lovely. If she doesn't listen, I'll send her away. She has to know it.

"Why?" she says.

Because history is a gazelle that is always with us. When Solomon was making plans to build a house for the Lord, and a house for his own kingdom, the planners he spoke with said they would cut wood in Lebanon and bring it to Joppa by the sea (2 Chron 2:16).

Sometimes, just after I returned to the earth from death, I could hear the shouts as they brought the trees to shore. I could hear them drag the trees to Jerusalem.

I think all of history trails behind us in a net.

I read her from another Scripture: "Jonah went to Joppa to find a ship to Tarshish" (Jonah 1:3).

"So ends the Scripture geography lesson for the afternoon," I tell the girl.

She hands me the cloth she has been working on.

Peter Calls Dorcas Back

"What happened?" I see the child's arm is bruised.

She got in the way of her mother, she tells me.

History is a place that heals us, I tell her.

There are old stories of Joppa. Once, it was walled. In the fifteenth century before Christ, Pharaoh Thutmose III and an Egyptian general named Thoth put two hundred soldiers in baskets carried by five hundred men. Thoth feigned surrender. "The baskets are filled with booty," he said. The gates of Joppa were opened.

The history of Joppa is old. Later, it fell to the Philistines, but the people prayed. In the second century before Christ, Simon—not the tanner, of course, but another one—wrestled it from the Syrians and annexed it to Judea.

Joppa is a rolling, rocky place. Our shallow bay is full of rocks that have fallen into the water through erosion from the hill.

"When we think of Joppa, we do not feel pain," I tell the girl. When we are Christians, the hurt is kept away.

I stand on the roof of my house at night and see the oil lamp burning at the tanner's, Simon's house. He and Peter are sharing their thoughts. Why don't they ask me to talk with them? Who do I have to talk to? The women who listen to nothing as they sew. I look to the sky and say, "Grandmother." My father's mother.

Maybe in heaven the clothes are given mouths.

What if all my sewing is waiting beyond what I had time to see when I was there. Or on the edge of there. Clothes that never wear out.

I am sewing closets for heaven where flying ephods land; I worship with my sewing.

Sometimes I see Peter talking to groups of men. The Hellenists. The Zealots. The shadow of the palm tree across Peter's striped tunic is like marks of waves in the sand. When I look at him, the sun fades everything in its light.

Sometimes, when I see Peter talking in the street, I go another way. If I see him walking, I step into a doorway until he passes.

Now it is the Gnostics I hear spouting. They would take away the garments the women sew. They dismiss our work as not counting for any spiritual good. Well, give them needles when they stand in line for heaven. Let them sew garments until they hear the threads speaking from their hands.

Now it is the commotion in the street that keeps Peter from seeing me. The sail-makers are carrying a sail to the ship in the harbor. The donkeys bray, protesting the weight. Everyone watches.

The crazy woman speaks like the donkeys.

The women are waiting for me when I return. Can't they sew without me? Am I the only one who has a house? Do they think I'd miss their talk?

"What is heaven like?" a few of them still ask.

But the closer I get, the less I can say.

A Chapter in Which an Afterword to Dorcas Continues

It was one of those rare evenings when I had people over for dinner. A colleague and his wife.

"I find the most interesting part of a project is the surprise. When something comes out of nowhere." Where was I going? I should stop talking. The wife wouldn't find it interesting. The colleague would. "I wanted to hear what she was thinking. I wanted her transfigured voice. I wanted to sew her story."

"Who?" asked the colleague.

"Dorcas," I answered. "I wanted to write about her as a woman who had a heart for others. I wanted her to talk about the tunics and garments she made, day after day, and how she made them. Can you imagine sitting in your office and finding all that? Or to know that someone who lived nearly two thousand years ago was in your mind? That you were writing her thoughts and experiences?"

No, my colleague could not—I saw by his face.

"I felt what her life was like in heaven . . ." It was a limited conversation. I seemed to be the only one talking. "Then I felt her return to earth. I could hear her voice as if from a little flock of goats."

The colleague and his wife only looked at me.

I continued thinking on my own: "The Scriptures were written by the inspiration of the Holy Spirit. The sixty-six books were gathered by the Nicene Council. Many books were left out. Those that did not contribute in a new way to the message, I suppose," I said, looking at the wife. "And many parts within the books, such as dialogue and the inner thoughts of people, are only mentioned."

Uprising of Goats

Sometimes when I read about the women in the Bible, I felt like I had the garment and not the person beneath it. I felt the same when I wrote about Dorcas. In spite of her benevolence, she kept herself to herself. In the end, what I might have had was not even a garment, but loose threads pulled from her unknown character.

"I am glad you have the strength to pursue your project," the colleague said as he left. "Others would have given up long ago."

I can't remember when I felt the little pain—the pain of religion, of puzzling over its truth, its necessity. It was enough for a life of study and absorption. But why not something more pertinent? Such as politics in the real world? Or the physical structure of the world? Or its theoretical physics? But it was belief that concerned me. I could sit through church nearly asleep, thinking of other things, and no one would ever know—except God, it dawned on me. Was I responsible for my thoughts? Yes, I decided. I wanted to explore faith even though I appeared unsophisticated to my colleagues. Someone to be dismissed. Why was I ostracized? Because I believed? Because I taught at a nominally Christian institution where the last thing welcome was talk of one's own Christian faith? Why did I not feel a part of everyone? I hardly realized it most of the time. I felt normal to myself. I was as I always had been. Was I just now seeing myself as others had seen me all along? I felt indignation. Anger. Was another voice upon me? These biblical women were doing me a favor. They got together to intercede. To share their battles with me. To let me know I wasn't alone. But this new voice was not going to get with the program. It had its own direction. It wasn't finished yet. Maybe the voice was a strainer for my voice. Maybe I would learn from it.

One weekend when my daughters were back from college, they wanted to go to the zoo. I wasn't sure why. We had not been to the zoo in a long time. It caught me off guard, but I didn't question them. For a moment, it seemed interesting to me also. As we walked past the monkey house toward the lions, I decided it was probably a final good-bye to their childhood.

In the aviary at the zoo, I saw birds with strange feathers on their heads. I made a note, thinking of what heaven would be like for Dorcas.

IV

Dorcas Returns from Death

...the fibre which Clotho packs the distaff for each one...
—Dante Alighieri, *The Divine Comedy*

When Peter is called away from Joppa, some of the men go with him. I watch him from the roof of my house. I do not think he looks up.

Peter walks as if he is a stone kicked from the hoof of a donkey. Or he walks as if he were the dust the wind swirls in the street, and then is gone.

"We must sew well," I tell the girl, looking at her crooked stitches. "An angel in heaven may wear what we sew."

I would like to have asked Cornelius what the angel wore.

I'm sure the Holy Spirit filled them with his tongues in Caesarea. I'm sure they run like gazelles on the plain.

The first fifty garments I make go to others. If I need needles, I give them away, then I sit in the sun flooding from my window. I wait in faith for more needles to come. Sometimes I see them float in through the light.

The girl waits until I am at a difficult place in my sewing to bother me.

"Dorcas?"

"What?"

"Can I come back in?"

"Take the bundle of fish bones to the dump."

"Then can I sew?"

"After I rest."

Do we ever leave anyplace we've been?

I watch a spider on the ceiling of my room crossing the surface of the water into heaven.

I think the people still talk when I pass.

Sometimes I remember my sickness. I look at the lamb and beef hanging in the market. I remember thinking, *How can I eat?* But I think about the Scriptures as I swallow.

Once, during a famine, Elisha's prophets found some wild vines and gourds in a field and sliced them into a stew. When they ate, they knew they were poisoned. But Elisha healed the prophets, and the stew, and they kept eating (2 Kgs 4:38–41).

Could I heal the cloth? The garments?

I can eat. I can clothe.

Thinking is sewing.

Sometimes when I hear the words of the Scriptures I feel like I am sewing. Somewhere in my head. The thoughts stitch themselves into the ear. The mind cuts them loose (to wear). They become the *chitones*, the *pepla*, the *himatioi* of the mind.

Have I said I am Hebrew and Gentile? The Gentile part is divided between those of faith and works.

I walk by the fish markets on the shore. I could step into the sea. I could sink like an underwater ship. I would frighten the fish.

Sometimes I don't eat. There is another kind of food. It comes through thought. I think that in the past, it has come in a time of famine. I am here on earth. I have arrived like a ship from afar. How dare Peter bring me back? How dare the other widows ask him to call me? I was in heaven. I was lifted out of Joppa as a bird. No, as a ship that could fly. Up through the clouds and through the sea on the other side of the sky. I was about to see the mysteries of the heavens. They were stepping out of the shadows, or maybe I was stepping out of the shadow world to them, after I got past my memorizing lessons.

Now I'm back in the dusty, lovely place: Joppa. Where Jonah sailed. Where Hiram of Tyre floated the cedars of Lebanon on their way to Jerusalem, to make Solomon's house and a house for the Lord.

Dorcas Returns from Death

Why couldn't they leave me alone? I was pulled back to a room where a man said, "Arise." He didn't even use my common name, Dorcas. Why didn't he bring someone else back, if he had to bring someone? Why not my husband? My little children? The man with a family? Someone who has something to do? A woman with small children?

What do I do now? Tolerate these women? Wait for another death?

How long am I here for now?

Why didn't they just meet in my house? Speak in memory of me. Did they have to send for Peter? Whose idea was it? Do I have to be here in person? I have the knowledge of heaven, but no one to whom I can speak. I have a language they can't understand. I still can't speak in tongues. I am more shut up than I was before. Don't they think about what they did? My needle does. I hear it more than ever now.

My foot still hurts. My camel-hoof foot. My toe could have been straightened. If God could raise me from the dead when Peter called my name, why can't my toe stop throbbing? My foot is a fisherman's boat that can't cross the sea. Was my toe crooked in heaven? Will it be straightened there? I was only there a short time. I didn't notice. But I don't think so.

Sometimes I remember the pain as if swallowing a needle. Sometimes I think my thoughts turn against me. I was there. I am here.

There was a sea of people and beings praising God. Their voices were waves. Heaven was noisy. There was sailing as though a ship arrived each day. Or logs on a float. Somehow, we should worship God. There were markets and wares and hawkers. I think there were magicians and traveling players. I think there were church meetings. I heard the different tongues I hear in Joppa. There were ladders and stone steps going up to another roof, and another roof, and up to a multitude of roofs like the waves I see stretching across the sea, and I knew they went on and on beyond that which I could imagine.

When they ask me, I say heaven was not one place, but many. Yet that doesn't say what I saw, but only something like it.

I tell them, "There are the last chapters of Ezekiel. The strange temple there. The closets. The storeys."

The memory of it is going farther away. "Don't go," I say to heaven. God is good; there is his goodness here. I must be satisfied where I am.

Uprising of Goats

I look at my chairs and table with a cruise of oil upon it. I look at my blanket and sewing closet, which I tell God was once a dry, covered room where I stored flour back when I still had meals to prepare for my family.

My house is his. I give it to God; we share it in common. I tell him to come into my (his) house. To sit by my (his) *oikas*.[1]

My needle is a gazelle through the cloth.

Peter annoyed me when he was in Joppa, but it was the way Christ thought that I liked.

Just imagine. My fingers are needles. Sewing is my atonement, my savior. My soul is a thought caught in the thinking. I would stand in the open on the roof of my house and not leave, but for the sun, the rain, the night air.

I embroider palmettes, rosettes. The girl embroiders with me. Sometimes I talk to her.

"God clothes the grass,"[2] the girl says. "Why doesn't he clothe his children?"

I look at her. "How can you say such things? Why do you question God? Look at those stitches. The mounds of threads you leave scattered on the floor. What can you do?"

"Who do you think cried for you to come back" she says to me.

My needle runs aground on my cloth. "What?"

She draws away from me. "I asked for you back. The women sent for Peter."

"Why did you do that?" I stick her with my needle.

She screeches. "They showed him the clothes you made."

This mystery life is. This needle through it.

I make myself memorize more Scripture. I buy more oil and sit by the lamp. I make the girl memorize too. She recites to me. I do not look at the tears on her face.

"Think of Joseph's coat," I say, "a tunic Jacob sewed for his son." Maybe it was like the bow after a rain, with red and the purple *tekhelet* from the sea mollusk, or a shadow of the sun on the sea, or the way a flame sometimes burns in a lamp—the way I feel different shades sometimes when I pull the thread through my fingers. Maybe Joseph's tunic was a shadow of heaven: transparent. You can see through heaven.

In heaven, words speak red and blue.

1. "Hearth."
2. Luke 12:28.

Dorcas Returns from Death

On earth, I sew sacks and pouches to stuff my feelings into.

Think how God clothes us with salvation. Think how he clothes the lilies (Luke 12:27).

We walk to the hill and watch the camel train arrive at Joppa. They are travelers coming in from the desert. They have walked a long way. I feel the momentum of their journey. Sometimes I think the camels don't want to stop. They could keep going across the sea if the men would let them. They stand in the marketplace, where everyone watches. They have carried their burdens. The rodents and vermin scurry. The pigeons and mourning doves fly. "Look at what they have done," I say to the girl. Just look.

The camels know we watch them. We can see the desert still on them like a cloak. They don't want to sit yet. They stand with their loads. The men try to get them to kneel. The camels protest. The men let them stand a while longer until the march across the desert fades, until they feel the stopping under their feet.

The girl and I listen to the merchants who have crossed the desert. We listen to the sailors who will take their goods across the sea. Even the camels say what they think.

The men argue about their ideas. The Stoics and Epicureans. But it is their feelings that show.

We watch the magicians in the marketplace.

The piles of goatskins for the tent-makers.

"God is no respecter of persons," Peter said when Cornelius sent for him (Acts 10:34). Maybe that's why he allows the girl to come into my house, though I pray against her. I put needles in her path. It is because I like to tell her what I think; it is because I have to do what God wants.

"He has clothed me with the garments of salvation" (Isa 61:10).

What is salvation? I have to get hold of my thoughts.

As for the madman, "Jesus clothed him in his right mind" (Mark 5:15).

Why didn't Peter heal the crazy woman, who stammers with her hair hanging in her face? Why didn't he heal the lepers? The blind? The crippled? The toothless? The ugly?

Peter is gone; the one who brought me back to life. It is hard to think he is not here. What if I need him again?

We begin to hear more about Saul, the persecutor of the Christians who was converted to Christianity. The men talk about him in the meetings of our *ekklesia*. I listen to their voices. Saul is now Paul. He-who-has-two-names goes many places. He is in Paphos, Perga, Pesidia. In the synagogues and churches.

At my house, the women talk about what we heard in *ekklesia*.

Paul is hearing the Jews argue with the believers. He is hearing the Jews, who are believers, say that the Gentiles have to become Jews before they can be Christians.

"You have to be born a Jew," a woman says as we sew.

"You can be circumcised and be a Jew," I say. "What's the difference?"

The woman looks at me, but doesn't answer.

I think sometimes Jesus is clothed with the moon, or that when it is full, it is a bright window he has opened to look at us.

I do not like Scriptures. There's a lot of tearing off and rending of clothes: David, Mordecai, Hezekiah, the prophets and priests. Was there one of them who didn't tear up their clothes?

When Paul and Barnabas were in Lystra, they called them Mercury and Jupiter. Paul and Barnabas then tore off their clothes and ran through the crowds crying, "We are men like you" (Acts 14:12–15).

Then Paul went to Troas. Neapolis. Philippi. Berea. Miletus. Ephesus. Perga. Attalia. Phenice. Samaria. Mysia. Bithynia.

None of them on the sea. None as lovely as Joppa.

What would all that traveling be like? What would it be like to flee? What does it mean that the Christian faith is built on moving? How would they like to sit in their house all day and sew?

The birds are chattering in the palm branches. There is a storm somewhere at sea; I feel the wind tugging it to shore. I tell the girl to stay with me. Maybe I should tell her there is a sermon at sea. What funny little seaworms the Scriptures are. I feel them coiling in my depths. They are solid as the cornerstone we set for the house.

The storm washes onto land by afternoon. It is more severe than I thought. I think of Simon, the tanner, who lives by the water. The path from God unto our city is wide as the sea. The girl and I embroider a gate to the sea. When the wind blows upon us, it is the girl's cloth that saves us. I see that now. God chooses the lowly things sometimes to teach us.

In my fear, I feel my mother swimming through the house in the storm. I cannot hold on. I put my face into the cloth. I could run faster than my mother on her crooked feet, until she caught me. I thrash as if I had

Dorcas Returns from Death

branches of the palm tree on my head. Why couldn't my father stop her? He always was busy with his work.

The girl sews while I cry. My feelings spill from the sacks and pouches I have made for them. I fear the cargo of feeling. It will not sink, no matter how hard I try to push it under the water. Will I have more Scriptures to learn? When I am in line getting ready for everything I learned? Will he listen to me? I hear a language in my mouth I had not heard. Sympathy for the girl.

After the storm, we walk through the soggy marketplace. We help the merchants pick up their wares. The meats and spices. Ruined. The grasshopper boxes. One crate with a dead chicken.

Would Peter have spoken the storm away? Rebuked it? Would the storm have listened? And obeyed?

The Stoics say the storm is something we have to bear. The Jews, who do not believe Jesus was the Son of God, say the storm is like the Gentiles who think they are grafted onto the vine of their God. The Hellenists speak of the storm in terms of a war among their Greek gods. The Christians try to explain the loss, but cannot.

We see the mess at Simon's house. His hides everywhere in a heap.

I see designs in the turmoil. I see patterns in the quiet that follows.

Simon tells us the crazy woman drowned in the storm. He found her on the shore by his house. I ask the men to carry her to my house.

The women wash her torn body. I push the hair back from her face and bind it with a thread, then embroider a few threads like storm clouds on her linen cloth. I see the sky is a cloth brought from far away.

The women cover her with spices and I close the seam with patterns of the quiet waves that follow the storm.

I stand at the crazy woman's tomb. I tell her to stay in line. Jesus will answer for her.

"But what if she wasn't saved?" the women ask. "What if the demons had her already, and won't let her go?"

There are some things that thoughts don't answer, but they are still more serviceable than the feelings.

Herod hates the *ekklesia*. We hear he kills the disciple James, the brother of John, in Jerusalem.

"Peter?" Simon asks anxiously.

Uprising of Goats

We hear that Peter is still alive in prison. Herod intends to kill him after Passover in front of the people. We pray for him in Joppa.

This blood religion. Yes, we are clothed in blood.

Then Simon, the tanner, tells us that Peter is out of prison. He says Peter was sleeping between two soldiers bound with chains, with guards at the door. He heard an angel say, *Peter, arise.* And his chains fell off his hands.

"*Arise*—that's what he said to me in the upper room of my house when he called my name," I say.

"The angel told him to get dressed and put on his sandals—maybe the sandals I made for him," Simon says, "and Peter followed the angel past the first and second guard, and when they came to the iron gate that leads to the city, the gate opened by itself."

Simon talks so fast I can hardly follow.

"When Peter got to the street, the angel was gone. Peter went to the house of Mary, the mother of John, where they were having a prayer meeting for him. Peter knocked at the door. A girl, Rhoda, came, but when she knew Peter's voice, she didn't open the door, but ran in and told them Peter was at the door. They said, "No, it was his angel." And Peter kept knocking, and finally they opened the door and let him in."

"Slow down, Simon," I say.

"Will Peter come here?" the girl asks.

Simon recovers his breath. "No," he answers. "He is traveling from Judea to Caesarea."

How do we sew what God is?

In the marketplace, we see the traveling players again.

At my house, we make a puppet for the girl. A likeness of herself: two legs, two arms. We could make the puppet an *euangelista*, I say. The girl laughs. We sew the puppet some teeth. But the girl wants me to use blue threads. We argue. I re-sew.

The teeth are uneven because I am impatient, and they are blue as the afternoon sea.

On the shore we look at shells. "We will use this pattern for the puppet's ears," I say. "If it is all right with you."

The girl looks at the shells. "The nose?" she asks, holding a long shell up for me to see.

Dorcas Returns from Death

"Nobody needs a nose," I tell her. "Just leave the mouth open and air can get in."

She laughs again. We walk on the shore, where we see tiny holes that bubble when the little waves retreat. "Eyes?" she asks.

"Yes, them. When I was dead I saw eyes in heaven." Sometimes the memory of heaven comes back like the small stitches I take in the cloth.

The eyes are everywhere, like little mounds of threads with holes in them—with caves in them.

"Everything gets into God's eyes," I tell the girl.

She shakes her head to show that she knows.

"God is full of eyes," I say again. He has no need of nostrils. But our eyes are dark ships with cargo holds where we put cloth.

The girl wants to name the puppet. I say it should not have a name. The girl disagrees. "Or we'll call her Hannah," I say, "Or a name I haven't thought of yet."

The girl calls the puppet a silly name, "Hannaput."

"No, only I can name it," I say. "Alright then, a puppet with two names. It has two legs, two arms, two thumbs on its fingerless hands, two eyes, two ears. Why not two names?"

"Should we make two mouths?"

"No, only one."

"There are two holes in our nose," the girl says, with her fingers in her nose.

I do not like to argue with her.

Now the girl sits with her hands in her lap. "Make it with a toe like yours," she says.

There are little closets in our head where we keep things. One head is enough. There is a little mouth that says things. One mouth is enough.

Later, I sew a tiny shell into the head for thoughts: a shell that coils like heaven, which must be in Jesus' head.

We name the puppet Hannaput, the daughter of Hannah. The daughter of Mary. The daughter of Elizabeth. The daughter of Ruth. The daughter of Leah. The daughter of Joanna. The daughter of Rachel. The daughter of Naomi. The daughter of Sarah. The daughter of Priscilla. The daughter of Lydia. The daughter of Deborah. The daughter of Timothy's mother. The daughter of Jael. The daughter of Abishag. The daughter of Phoebe. The daughter of Rahab. The daughter of Martha. The daughter of Jezebel. The daughter of Rebekah. The daughter of Susanna. The daughter of Anna. The daughter of Dinah. The daughter of Esther. The daughter of the nameless women. All daughters of Eve.

When the puppet dies, we lay it on the table and wrap it in cloth. The girl is the apostle who raises the puppet from the dead.

"What is it like to come back from the dead?" I ask the puppet over and over.

The girl sends her voice into a corner of the room, but the puppet's teeth are shut like the old gates of Joppa. I have pulled the threads too tight.

The girl cannot pound open the mouth, that ship from far away with its cargo in its belly. The girl plays with the puppet more than she sews.

I say, "I have to put the puppet under the grinding stone when the miller isn't looking."

"No, no!" the child screams.

But I insist. "We have to lose what we are," I tell her.

The girl begs, but I do not listen.

The donkey pulls the stone across the puppet.

The girl will not speak to me.

We embroider.

We walk along the sea. We see the merchants who come to Joppa from the desert; we see the captains who come to land from the sea. We copy the patterns of palm fronds; we copy the light in the water that is pulled from the well.

The *euangelista* who run from persecution stay with Simon and the others before they leave on the trading ships. They bring us news.

In *ekklesia*, we hear that Saul, whose name is Paul, went to Jerusalem to see Peter. But later, when Peter went to Antioch, we hear they did not get along. Peter would eat with the Gentiles, but when the Jews came, Peter withdrew and would not eat with them.

I see Simon has cleaned the mud from his house. I see how much he has lost after the flood.

"How can you not be consistent?" Paul asked Peter.

We hear it was no small argument.

"If Peter thought he was justified by faith, why was he relying on works?" someone asks.

"Because we have to work," I say. What else is there to do? It is the fulfillment of belief.

Dorcas Returns from Death

Why was Peter unclear as to what to do? What was the matter with him? Didn't he have a vision?

My needle is my consecration. Just give me a few threads. There is a holiness so bright in the sewing. Only sewing reaches the kingdom of heaven.
 A word leaving the mouth is a thread pulled through the cloth.
 Sewing is the flame from the oil lamp. The night *wools* on my bed.
 Kurios,[3] I call, sewing his hands to the sky. Sometimes I want him to take me back; I want my gazelle feet. Then I feel panic because Peter is gone.
 Savior of sewing. Savior of light.

I watch the sailors unload an *othone*.[4]
 Be careful, I think.
 I see the patterns I will sew along the seams of the tunics. I see the islands and countries between them. A flock of starlings circling over.
 Why do we live? To think of ideas of why we live. The thoughts in the many-ideaed place of Joppa, a seaport town where cargo moves between the water and the land. The camels unload their cargo. O Jerusalem, a day's journey over the hill, where the camels head with their cargo just arrived from the sea, passing through Joppa, which is a border between—through the houses and streets, the sun-caked marketplace. And God like a donkey to cart us to the sea.
 I think of God clothed in the mast of the sea. I would ask what clothes God wears. I almost saw him once. Surely he has changes.
 The waves embroider their little ridges on the shore. Sometimes I think the fish sew.
 That night, the quarter moon is like the jagged edge of a broken tooth. I think of the crazy woman we buried, of how we closed her mouth.
 I am a crooked-toed old woman wrapped with my sewing. I would be nothing, but for Jesus. And my sewing.

The girl carries my basket for me to the marketplace. When she sees a puppet, she says nothing. I know she is thinking of Hannaput.
 I see a sailor split open his leg on a nail. I could take my thread and needle and sew him up, if someone would hold him. The opening will ooze,

---

3. "Lord."
4. "Sheet of linen."

Uprising of Goats

and even the salt will not keep out death. It will enter him, has already, along the open shaft of his leg. I could bind the leg with cloth, but the cloth would sink into the wound.

Simon and the Christian men pray. *Euchontai.*[5] *Euchai.*[6]

I do not think the sailor will survive. He will cross the water to heaven, where I've been.

These are the ways of thinking, I tell the girl. It is what my grandmother taught me.

Dokein. To form an opinion, which can be either right or wrong. Or both, when considered from different viewpoints.

Hegeisthai. To conclude.

Noein. To perceive. Understand. Apprehend. To think differently afterwards.

Huponoein. To surmise.

Nomizein. To suppose.

Logizrsthai. To reckon by calculation or imputation. *Kataxiousthai.* To count.

Exouthenein. To make no account.

Oiesthai. To imagine. *Phainein.* To form an opinion.

Epiballein. To throw oneself upon.

I repeat the ways of thinking to the girl. I think of other words for thought that my grandmother taught me. "We live to think what we know," I tell the girl.

Phronein. Axioun. Enthumeisthai. Huperphronein. Dienthumeisthai.

The ways of thinking are nearly limitless.

"I still have not told you all," I tell her.

The girl falls at my feet as though dead. But she is acting.

I will give her to the traveling players, I tell her. She can be their puppet and ride over the desert on a camel. And sleep on the sand. And eat lizards that are tough as Simon's leather from being in the sun.

I see that she is thinking. "You will dry like a fig. Your skin will darken." I see she looks at me. "Your eyes will yellow like mustard and saffron."

The girl holds her fingers in her ears.

I ask about the sailor when I am in the marketplace.

---

5. "They pray."
6. "The prayers."

Dorcas Returns from Death

He is on a ship. They carried him on a litter, though I think it should be a bier.

Now the ship is ready to sail.

What would I tell him about dying if I had spoken? God clothes himself with words. Start memorizing Scripture. I think you will need it there.

"These are the ways of reasoning," I tell the girl. At times, she seems to listen. I mention her name in *ekklesia*. The men pray for her.

When I pray for her, I think of having patience.

Dialegesthai. To think different things with oneself.

Dialogizesthai. To bring together different reasons.

Sullogizesthai. To compute.

Suzetein. To examine. Discuss. Dispute.

The girl runs from the *ekklesia*.

In *ekklesia*, I request prayer for the girl again.

We hear that Paul, whose name was Saul, is in Ephesus.

I hear my needles call from the bottom of the sea as if they were the cargo ship that sank. Thoughts are bright needles that get us through this life. They are a fish-knife splitting the fish.

"Has Simon heard from Peter?" a woman asks as we sew at my house. Sometimes, they remember when he brought me back to life.

"He asked Jesus to bring me back to life," I correct them.

They look at me, but I don't have any words about death to tell them. Words have never been mine; they are strangers when I speak, a wind that should have brought a storm. If the words form in my mouth, my thoughts shut them down. It is better to be quiet. Maybe it's my thoughts that get in my way. I poke them with my needle to see if I am better without them also.

If only I had seen rolls of linen in heaven. If only I knew they were there. I could say I saw one hundred spools of thread. Ten cases of needles. Ornaments of coral and pearl. I could say I saw parchments with drawings of cloaks and shawls and belts and tunics. The sun danced on them between the palm fronds, juggling its light. I want to know I can sew more tunics before they are turned into ephods. But there are no words for what I saw in heaven. Rolls of scrolls on the shelves. Fields, mountains, and seas of people praising God. Creatures I have never seen. I cannot link. Sometimes my thoughts of heaven make me shudder.

I still can't eat figs. They remind me of leaches that swim in the water. If the women ask me again, I will say, "I don't feel changed by death."

Uprising of Goats

For all I know, I am still dead. Maybe there is no difference.

I think dying is slipping into heaven as if it were the sea. But the sea is a priest's ephod with its blue robe. There is a hole in the top of it, and a binding of woven work around the hole, as if for coat of mail, such that it cannot be rent. The priest's ephod and its robe are like the sea with a hole to fit the head into.

The sea is entering the moving garment of heaven, flowing on its journey, changing with thought, built upon what we know on earth of God, what we're aware of, what we think, how our thoughts form a relationship to God through Jesus. That's what Jesus wants of us: our thoughts, which are jugglers. Maybe the purpose of life is to make the ephod we wear with him in heaven.

I sit in my house after the women are gone. What should I do now that I am back from death? Sometimes there is such loveliness in lighting the fire and cooking the barley cakes in olive oil. I do what I have to do here in my house. The ordinariness of it: the loveliness, loveliness. The camel trains and ships do not know I am here, yet I have been farther than they have. Maybe death is just another journey, getting up, walking through the door and out across the water under the firmament into heaven. If Christ be the place they want to go.

In *ekklesia*, I hear another Scripture. When Jeremiah was in the dungeon, worn garments were used to make cords to lift him (Jer 38:11–13). I could have told them that. It's clothes that pull us up.

Jesus, the resurrector of our cloth.

Even women could be priests like Samuel and Aaron. Hadn't I thought so in heaven? Hadn't I seen the holy garments? The closets of coats, the robes of the ephod, the ephods, the breastplates, girdles, and the mitres, which are the thoughts embroidered in the head. Weren't they for all? Women the same as men.

In the end, if they keep bothering me, I will tell them, "It is the self alone that survives."

"In the end," I will tell them, "it's what we sew."

A Chapter in Which an Afterword to Dorcas Ends

Bless Justine Crowd, my colleague and rival who taunted me with remarks she knew I could hear. Bless each student who went to her office to hear her blasphemy. Maybe I was going too far. How could I return anything from the Bible that didn't sound mindless? Faith and reason often didn't mix. Maybe never mixed. But postmodernism was in. There was no division between right and wrong, good and bad, only the way it was perceived. Everything was relative. Everything was smeared together. The more I read Scripture, the more I felt that God was not postmodern. I remembered the story of Lazarus and the rich man—not Lazarus, the brother of Mary and Martha, but Lazarus the beggar, who died and was comforted while the rich man went to a torment from which there was no escape. That story was in the sixteenth chapter of Luke. Maybe I could post that note on Justine Crowd's door.

During lunch, I made another note and put the paper back in my purse. I had a thought I didn't want to forget.

"Was it something I said?" a colleague asked.

"Close to it."

Surely he knew I had thoughts different from what was going on. Why was I holding back?

But I couldn't speak openly of the voices.

As a child, I had always liked the story of the three little pigs. If the wolf asked what time the pigs were going to town, and they were going at noon, the pigs answered, "One o'clock," so that they would have already passed the road where the wolf waited. How deceitful, the little pigs.

And why would my new book be about the voices of biblical women? Not the book that was an accumulation of my lectures, but my new book in progress.

Why not a literary voice? Why not a saint, if it had to be religious? Or something more relevant, I asked myself again. I argued with Dorcas for a long time. I asked her to go away, but she kept talking. I told her a biblical voice would not go over in academia, though with tenure I could do what I wanted. It was still a thought I was getting used to—possible tenure. But the underside—no tenure when I would be turned away from the college—was also a possibility. I woke sometimes in the middle of the night with the weight of insecurity.

I had tried to push Dorcas aside, but she would not move. I found I could work on her voice while writing my own lectures or grading papers. Maybe the uncertainty of my situation threatened her story.

"You seem busy with your thoughts," a colleague said at the faculty table as we ate.

"Yes, I'm thinking about something I am working on," I answered. "I've seen you do the same."

I ate out almost every evening. I would leave my office at six-thirty. Sometimes I would meet someone in the parking lot and decide where to go for dinner. Usually I ate alone with a book or a paper I had yet to read. Often, I didn't have the time or inclination to cook, though of course from time to time I did, but I liked eating out. I could almost afford it. My daughters were in college. I was no longer married. The divorce was nearly final. My students, my teaching, my research, my projects—they were my children now. Mostly, I liked to eat alone, looking over my notes as I ate.

I had gone to church since I was a child. I still attended. It was something I both needed and wanted to do. My college also recommended attendance, though not everyone went. I had stood at my father's bed when he died. I wanted to call after him, asking where he had gone. It seemed like there was a passing above—my mother thought so too. It was the same a few years later when she died. I don't know how else to say it. There was a destination toward which they were headed. I felt left out. I was saddened because I didn't get to go, despite the differences I had with them.

A Chapter in Which an Afterword to Dorcas Ends

Like a broken tooth and a foot out of joint.

—Prov 25:19

One morning, I sat at the breakfast table with a plate of fruit. The sliced kiwi's symmetrical seeds radiated outward from the white center to the green. But the outside of the kiwi was like goatskin.

Several times I missed faculty and department meetings. Several times I simply was more interested in having time to work on the voices of the Biblical women than in tolerating the opinions of my colleagues on matters that did not interest me as much as the voices. How did Dorcas get used to life the second time? What was it like to be sucked back? As if the first wasn't enough. How did she handle her letdown?

I had to give the department the names of courses I wanted to teach in the fall and send a list of my required books to the bookstore so they could be ordered. I had to fill out different forms for teacher's copies. It was always time-consuming. I had returned from death and was standing on the far edge of Dorcas' life, and the department coordinator wanted something that had nothing to do with what I was working on. I would have to go to the bookstore and the library. I wanted to look at the books in print, especially at forthcoming books. I couldn't teach the same books each semester. I had to keep changing them to keep myself interested, and therefore the students.

I made notes for new courses: "The History and Practice of Christianity." "Faith and Religious Identity." "The Making of Old and New Testament Texts." Maybe "The Household of Christianity." I always wanted to teach a course titled "Jesus Is Real." It was my colleague, Justine Crowd, who often said within hearing that Jesus was an imaginary friend that some people did not outgrow. This was the Religion Department in a Christian college, after all, and I could not mention the blunt fact that I was a Christian. Can you imagine? I was growing cranky as Dorcas.

MICHAL

A Stone I Could Not Lift
A Chapter Found on the Slope of a Steep Hill

And Saul saw and knew that the Lord was with David, and that Michal, Saul's daughter, loved him.

—1 SAM 18:28

I DIDN'T LIKE THE prophet Samuel. He said my father was rejected by God. My father was the first king over Israel, and Samuel talked to him like that. Just because my father used his own judgment. He had to do what was expedient. The Philistines came for war—the men of Israel saw they were hedged in. They hid in caves and thickets. They hid among the rocks and in the hills. Where was Samuel? My father waited a week before he made the burnt offering that had to be made before battle.

"What have you done?" Samuel asked my father when he finally arrived.

"The Philistines gathered, the people were scattered, and you did not come at your appointed time," Saul answered.

"The Lord God would have established your kingdom," Samuel replied, "but now he will not."

Just because my father acted as a priest when none was there? What was he supposed to do?

A Stone I Could Not Lift

We heard the battle from camp. The women and children sat together, some of us silent, some of us crying. The watchmen shouted; the garrisons moved back and forth across the field. The ground seemed to tremble. We felt it under our feet. Was it an earthquake? There was confusion and panic. My mother Ahinoam and my sister Merab cried for Saul and his sons, Jonathan, Ishvi, and Malchishua. Then the watchmen shouted that the Hebrews routed the Philistines that day. The scribes wrote what the watchmen said. Were they writing that my father was rejected? Were they writing what I thought?

Oh, what did he do then? How did Saul, my father, offend Samuel next?

Samuel also said to Saul, "The Lord sent me to anoint you king over his people, over Israel: now therefore hearken to the voice of the words of the Lord. Thus said the Lord of Hosts, 'Remember that which Amalek did to Israel, how he laid wait for him in the way, when he came up from Egypt. Now go smite Amalek, and utterly destroy all that they have, and spare them not; but slay both man and woman, infant and suckling, ox and sheep, camel and ass'" (1 Sam 15:1–3).

There was an old passage: "Remember what Amalek did to you by the way, when you were come out of Egypt; how he met you by the way, and smote those behind you, even all that were feeble, when you were faint and weary; and he did not fear God. Therefore it shall be, when the Lord your God has given you rest from all your enemies, in the land which the Lord your God has given you for an inheritance, that you will blot out the remembrance of Amalek from under heaven; do not forget it" (Deut 25:17–19).

But Saul spared Agag, the Amalekite, and the best of the sheep and oxen and lambs. Who wouldn't? My father was king. He made his own decisions.

"What is this bleating of sheep I hear?" Samuel asked when he came on another circuit from Ramah to Bethel to Gilgal to Mizpah to Ramah.

"I was going to sacrifice them to the Lord," my father answered.

"Obedience is better than sacrifice," Samuel said, and he ripped the shirt my father wore and said the kingdom of Israel was torn from him.

I saw those scribes writing everything down. I would eat the scribes' parchment if I could. I would drink their ink. I would hide their writings forever!

Samuel didn't come back to my father after that.

Uprising of Goats

There were hard days of fighting the Philistines. They stood on one side of a hill, and our men stood on another with the valley between them, until a man went out. Not just any man—a giant. He taunted the Hebrews, who were afraid of him. But David ran out and slung a stone and the giant fell.

Jonathan, my brother, brought David to our house. Jonathan gave him his own garments, his own sword and bow. They were inseparable. My sister Merab and I watched them. David went wherever my father sent him. When they returned from defeating the Philistines, the women sang, "Saul has slain his thousands, and David his ten thousands."

Those were hard days. There were other battles with the Philistines. My father was unsteady. Irrational. But he was king—I thought I heard someone say that Samuel had anointed David as king, but I didn't care. No one did. But sometimes I saw my father watch David. One night, we were talking after dinner when suddenly, unexpectedly, Saul threw a javelin at him. My father missed, and David ran. I thought he would not be able to come back—yet Saul promised Merab, my sister, to David. What was my father thinking? I wanted David!

I ran to my father, "Promise me to David!" I pleaded.

Just before the wedding, he gave Merab to Adriel, the Meholathite.

There would be a wedding. But it wasn't the wedding of Merab and David! She didn't seem displeased. She seemed to like Adriel as much as David. I was giddy at Merab's wedding. Even my mother pulled me aside. The feasting and the dancing. The drink and the merriment. I would be David's wife, though my father gave me to David as a snare. Saul asked David to fight more Philistines and bring one hundred foreskins to Saul. My father thought David would be killed by the Philistines. And if he lived, he would have my temper to deal with. But David brought my father the foreskins. The upstart David would have a king's daughter for a wife.

Merab was promised to David, but Saul gave her to Adriel. I was married to David—after he killed the Philistines.

There is nothing like the wedding of a king's daughter. Merab and my handmaids helped me prepare. They washed me in fragrant oils. I met David in glorious wedding garments. The house was decked in flowers. The musicians played. I was delirious. I was a king's daughter. I received many gifts.

My father grew jealous of David. He sent messengers to our room to watch him. I knew my father would try to kill him.

"Run! You have to run," I told David. I let him down through a window, and he fled. I made a bolster of goat hair and placed it in his bed. The messengers came into the room. "He is sick," I told them. They stood at the door and saw his likeness in bed.

"He is sick," I said when Saul sent the messengers again, but they uncovered the bed.

Who knows where David went after he fled. Jonathan, my brother, knew. Jonathan was always with David. I couldn't go into battle. I couldn't follow after him. I couldn't speak to David like a man did. I stayed with the women—the little flock of goats. I waited in the tent until he came to me. I was afraid of my father. An evil spirit bothered him. Sometimes David played his harp, and my father was himself again. My sister was going to have a child already. Maybe that will be next for me. Jonathan told me that David was with Samuel, but he didn't tell me where. Ramah, I supposed. The new moon was upon us. We all came to dinner in Saul's house. David was not there. He was not missed by my father.

The next night, David's place was still empty. My father asked Jonathan where David was. "Bethlehem," Jonathan answered. But I did not believe it. Saul did not believe Jonathan either, and he threw a javelin at Jonathan, and Jonathan ran.

I didn't have time to tell him, "Take me with you." Why was I married if not to be with my husband? Merab was with Adriel.

David lived in a cave. The men came to him. Everyone in distress, everyone in debt, everyone discontented. He became captain over these—David's mighty army.

I paced my father's house. I was wild as a goat that jumped the rocks. Marriage to David wasn't what I thought. I wanted to ride through the marketplace with him. I wanted David to play his harp at my knee. I wanted my father to hear him and be soothed again. But that would not happen. Instead, I went to live with Merab, my sister.

My father went after David every day. He did not let up. He was as relentless as the Philistines. Nothing I could do would stop him.

I heard David was here. He was there. He was fighting the Philistines. He was running for his life from my father. All the while, I held Merab's son.

Uprising of Goats

Then I heard he had another wife, Abigail. Then another. And another. Did David ever think of me? Did he know I was with Adriel and Merab?

In anger, Saul, my father, gave me to Palti, son of Laish, from Gallim. He had always wanted me. So had others. I was a king's daughter. I cried at the wedding. Merab stood with me. Palti told me he had cried when I married David. I was cared for in Palti's house. I was doted on. Why was I not happy?

Then David had another wife, and another, and another.

The prophet Samuel died, but not before anointing David to be king over Israel. My father, seeking direction in despair, called upon the witch of Endor. She called up Samuel, still an old, stooped man. "What do you want?" Samuel asked, irritated that he'd been called up from the dead.

"The Philistines make war again," Saul said.

"What can I do?" Samuel said. "Why do you ask me, seeing the Lord has departed from you? The Lord has torn the kingdom out of your hand. He will deliver Israel into the hand of the Philistines." The prophet Samuel, always spilling over with good news.

The Philistines fought hard, and the men of Israel fled. The Philistines followed Saul and his sons. They killed Jonathan, Ishvi, and Malchishua. Then the archers lifted their bows against Saul and wounded him severely. Saul asked his armor-bearer to draw his sword and kill him. He didn't want to be killed by the Philistines, but the armor-bearer would not.

Then Saul, my father, fell on his own sword because his armor-bearer would not kill him. When the armor-bearer saw that Saul was dead, he killed himself too.

Merab and I cried with grief as we heard the news.

The Philistines found the bodies of my father and three brothers. They cut off my father's head and sent it into the land of the Philistines as a trophy. They put his armor in the house of Ashtaroth and fastened his body to the wall of Bethshan. When the Jabesh-Gileads heard what the Philistines did to Saul, they went at night for the bodies of Saul and my brothers. They took them to Jabesh and burned them there, then buried their bones under a tree.

Merab and I mourned while the baby cried. Was there nothing to appease the child? I handed him back to the nurse. I went to my chamber and wept.

A Stone I Could Not Lift

In the years to come, Merab had two more sons. We told the children stories of their grandfather, Saul. He killed Gibeonites. He fought against Moab and Ammon, against Edom and Zobah, against Amalekites and Philistines.

The Philistines had the ark. I'm not sure what difference it made. No, I did know. It marked the presence of God.

I was a king's daughter. I received many gifts. Grief. Rage.

When my father died, Abner, the commander of my father's army, wanted to join with David. Abner would be leader of Judah. David would be the leader of Israel. David said, "Give me my wife, Michal, to whom I was married at the price of one hundred foreskins."

When I heard the news, I was angry. Would I take my place in line with the other wives? When I went to back to David, Palti, my husband, followed me weeping all the way to Bahurim, where Abner told him to leave. It was not me that David wanted, but the power of the house of Saul, the first king of Israel.

I lived in David's house. Room after room. Wives. Concubines. Children. Children. None of them mine.

My sister had a fourth son. She sent messengers for me. I visited her often, but this time, she was troubled. She was weak and could not play with the children. I sent for the children. I held them. Ran with them. I was in the house of Adriel as much as the house of David. I took over what Merab could not do. I directed the household tasks. I instructed the children. I told my nephews more stories of Saul, their grandfather, sometimes repeating the ones they wanted to hear. When they were older, I would tell them all the stories.

David gathered thirty thousand men and went after the Philistines again. He took the ark back from the Philistines and brought it back to the city of David. When the ark of the Lord came into the city, I looked from the window of David's house at the noise. I saw David leaping and dancing. I despised him. Where did he come from that he danced that way in view of everyone? Did he think he was still in the sheep-pasture where no one could see? Didn't he know he was in the court of Israel? Didn't he know his father-in-law was the first king of Israel?

I went out to meet him and saw him dancing before the ark almost naked. How glorious was the king of Israel today, who uncovered himself in the eyes of the handmaids of his servants, as one of the vain fellows shamelessly uncovering himself.

David looked at me. "I dance before the Lord, who chose me as ruler over all the people. I will yet me more contemptible than this. I am willing to be base in my own sight; and of the maidservants of whom you have spoken, of them shall I be had in honor" (2 Sam 6:20–22).

A prophet came to me that afternoon and told me I would be barren the rest of my life. Are they writing it down? The scribes, Seraiah and Sheva, those ones who write? Jehoshaphat and the recorders also take notes. I want to say what they don't say—what they leave out.

My sister drew close to delivery of yet another child. She dreamed she was watching a goat climb a high rock. She heard its bell. Then she heard nothing. She called, but the goat did not return. She was despondent, and I tried to encourage her. She died when the child was born. It was not unexpected. I asked to stay in Adriel's house and raise my sister's five children. David hardly knew I was gone. I was David's wife. He had married the daughter of the first king of Israel. The kingdom was all his. That was what mattered to him.

I lived in Adriel's house, not as a wife, but as a mother to Merab's children. I thought in time Adriel would take another wife, and if he did, she would have her own children. Merab's children were now my own. I walked with them through the marketplace. I sat next to them on holy days. I called them mine. They were grandsons of a king. They drove away the shame of not having children of my own.

Then there was famine in Israel. We pounded gritty meal. Our flocks withered. Our stomachs hurt with hunger. Nothing would grow because of drought. We had eaten everything we could. There was nothing ahead but more hunger. Children and the old ones died. We grew weak. We were sick. What if the Canaanites attacked? What if they made a league with enemy tribes and vagabonds? But they were hungry too, Adriel assured us. They would not have the strength.

I stole the last of the grain from the storehouses to feed the boys. I got on my knees and picked up pieces from the ground with my fingers.

After the third year of famine, David asked the Lord the reason for the famine. The Lord favored David. He always did. David had committed more sins than my father. My father didn't take another man's wife. He didn't send Uriah, the woman's husband, to the front line to be killed. But the Lord answered David. The famine was because of the Gibeonites that Saul had killed. The Gibeonites had come to Saul because they heard how their God led Israel from Egypt. They asked to be servants. Joshua made peace with them. He made a league with them and let them live. But Saul had broken that league.

David asked the Gibeonites what he could do.

"Let seven men of Saul's sons be hanged," they said.

David and his men came for my sister's five sons. I screamed in their faces. I had raised the boys. Don't take them! They carried my father's stories. They carried our heritage. I hardly knew what they were doing. Adriel knew before I did and tried to stop them, but David's men held him back. I saw then what was happening. I cried like a goat. My hooves clattered the floor. My horns rammed the wall. But David took the five sons of Merab, whom I had brought up for Adriel, and he took Armoni and Mephibosheth, the two sons of Rizpah, the daughter of Aiah, whom she bore to Saul, and delivered them into the hands of the Gibeonites. They hanged them on the hill before the Lord. They fell, all seven together, put to death in the beginning of barley harvest—I lay on the ground before them, unable to rise.

How could the Gibeonites, those servants, do that?

I screamed the names of my nephews—they were nearly my sons—Kishani, Joniathan, Saulali, Aphiniah, Bechor. Do you think I would use their actual names so they could be derided? I use these names for bolsters—made to look as though they were their names. I screamed at the scribes not to write their names. Those poachers. The names of my nephews would not be known. They would not be dishonored.

The house of Adriel was in mourning. Their father was inconsolable. He could not eat. I finally put a piece of bread to his mouth and he took it. I wiped the drool that came from his mouth.

I think fury kept me alive. I pushed my hands to my eyes until I saw my rage white as goat's milk. I was caught on the prong of God—and I was supposed to praise him?

I was David's first wife. Were any of his other wives the daughter of a king? How could he destroy his father's-in-law house? Why didn't he hang me?

Uprising of Goats

Afterward, in her uprising, Rizpah, who lost only two sons, took sackcloth and spread it upon the rock, from the beginning of harvest until water dropped upon us out of heaven, and allowed neither the birds of the air to rest on them by day, nor the beasts of the field by night (2 Sam 21:10).

For weeks, I cried at Merab's grave. The end of my efforts was grief. Maybe Merab had welcomed her sons into death—into whatever darkness was there. Maybe they were with our father and brothers. No, none of us went anywhere.

I walked through the marketplace again as a barren woman. I remembered Samuel's words to my father: "Now go your way and you will meet a group of prophets coming down from a hill with psaltery and timbrel and flute and harp and they will prophesy. And the spirit of the Lord will come upon you, and you will prophesy with them, and shall be turned into another man."

I was born into a king's house. Now I was a goat. I had been turned into another. I heard the wind whistle in the hills, answering my bellowing.

These words stayed with me. These goat-cries in my throat. "And the spirit of the Lord will come upon you and you will be turned into another" (1 Sam 10:6). I swept the hills. Inconsolable. I wandered in the rocks wild with rage. I had lost David, my husband. He was full of other wives. I had lost my father, my brothers, my sister, my nephews, my whole house. I had seen my nephews, who had inherited the blood of a king, taken to the gallows. They had grown into tall young men, some hardly more than boys. I licked the rock with my tongue. I sat as though dead. My grief was a Goliath before me. All I had was a rock I could not lift.

I thought of David's passions, his exuberances, his despondencies, his irritating ways. He threw himself against God. He sought God, which my father had not. David threw himself against a rock. *The* rock, I suppose I could say. My father ruled as a king should rule. David ruled as a shepherd would rule, throwing stones at wolves, hearing the wind sweep over the land, unaware of anyone watching him—other than God, of course. David played his flute and wrote his dripping words. He destroyed my life and the lives of my nephews. I can say he killed my father also because Saul knew David had replaced him while he yet ruled. But I had been a reproach to

David. I had caused him a little grief, but not as much as I wished I had. My father was right. I would be a snare—though David would brush that aside too. I think his only punishment was that he didn't get to build the temple he wanted to build.

I traveled to the sepulcher of Kish, my grandfather, to visit the bones of Saul and my brothers, Jonathan, Ishvi and Malchishua, and to swallow more grief for my nephews.

What could I do with my anger? How could I hold my devastation? I lost my nephews because of my father's impulses. Why had Saul not thought? Why did he not know about the league with the Gibeonites? Had he slept through the reading of the scrolls of our history? Or did he know and killed the Gibeonites anyway? My father did not think beyond himself. He thought he knew what he should do. He was the one to decide. The only ideas he had were of what he thought he should do. I had continued his lineage. Not with children; no, I had no children. I had been judged by God because I chided David when he danced before the Lord. I carried my father's attitude. I never was anything but an idea of what I was. I saw myself in the king's house. Could I ever stop and think? Could I ever understand? Could I think about what another felt or thought? Even God? Was it worse than what David had done? We had all made mistakes. What had I learned from this loss and sorrow? For a moment, I wished I could hear that old prophet Samuel's voice. I would say, "I learned I shouldn't cross God." I learned that if I did, I would have the kingdom ripped from my hands. I would have my children killed. I would live in desolation. I would see my enemies ruling. Their children would be in line for the kingdom. I stood at my father's sepulcher. I fell on the ground and wept. I said like Jacob, "God was in this place, and we never knew it."

A Chapter in Which There Is an Afterword to Michal

I often say, "Our work is a scream of freedom."
—Christos

Michal, ca. 19 bc.

He was small and ruddy. I thought he was swift. I was the king's daughter. I could have who I wanted. These were the words I heard from Michal, first wife of David. I never cared for apologetics, but that's what I was writing.

I sent the pieces out for publication once again. I received them back. I had a world I had to hide. It hawked me. It felled my sky. It overshadowed my field. Its shadow left a black hole.

Walker was dating a woman, of course. The girls told me. Did I expect him to remain alone? Did I expect to stay alone? No, but that's how it was. I was on the edge of desperation and frustration as I waited for the tenure committee to make their decisions. I felt the removal of another security, though I didn't hope the marriage to Walker would renew itself.

Early in the spring semester, I went to an academic conference. I took a side trip to the Gulf. One night I heard the goats. It might have been waves or the wind that lifted in a brief storm. I got up and went to the window. Afterwards, I sat in a chair in the dark and tried to write in the dim light of the window.

A Chapter in Which There Is an Afterword to Michal

    I was not a king's daughter, but I had my hand in the bee's nest before I knew it—my hand in the part of the world with a stinger. Had not a hornet nest brought the family down? This is not a world for peace. There is no softness in the center. It takes war in the heart to live. It took a horrid death on the cross to atone—a torture chamber like those regimes stuffed in the newspaper somewhere between recipes and local news.

    I felt Michal's rage. I felt her grief that was beyond bearing. Still, another voice was coming. Sometimes they were hard to hear. Other noises in the way seemed to be interference instead of accompaniment. In places, my voice seemed to slip into theirs, or theirs into mine. I wanted to call them back as they had been. They were a cloud of witnesses. They lessened the distance between then and now. The women seemed to live when I worked with their voices. I wanted to call them like a flock of goats. But did goats come when they were called?

    In the upheaval of the spirit—in the struggle to do my work, to stay afloat in academia, and possibly in the world of biblical women—the struggles became a causeway of voices from one place to another. In my powerlessness, I could hear their powerlessness.

    Later that night, I had a dream. The goats I called were wearing dresses. They were hanged on a gallows, their bare feet sticking out beneath their dresses.

When the girls called with a minor crisis, I made a trip to visit them.

    Oh leave me. Do not leave me. I was crushed with work. I was hampered with worry. I could not rise from my desk, though it was time for another class when I returned to my college.

    After the class, another student knocked on the door. These interruptions. These intrusion into the text of the message. These women's voices. This marginal writing. No, the students were the crux of my work. I let them into my office. I sat listening to them while the voices waited for me to return to them. I let them graze in the pasture I wanted for myself.

    In the next weeks, there was a leaving off. An opening to the next testament. Where else did I have to go? Another voice was making its journey toward me.

ANNA

A Chapter in Which a Raisin Cake Is Wrapped in Cloth

Now there was one, Anna, a prophetess, the daughter of Phanuel, of the tribe of Asher. She was of a great age, and had lived with a husband seven years from her virginity; and this woman was a widow of about eighty-four years, who did not depart from the temple, but served God with fastings and prayers night and day. And coming in that instant [when Simeon recognized the child Jesus in the arms of Mary] she gave thanks likewise to the Lord, and spoke of him to all those who looked for redemption in Jerusalem.

—Luke 2:36–38

Just before Christmas, the pastor at our church was talking about Simeon and Anna. He said that Anna must have led a lonely life in the temple. He saw her languishing for eighty-four years. I was working on Anna's voice at the time. She seemed full of life to me. She couldn't wait to pray. I wanted to raise my hand and disagree with the pastor.

A Chapter in Which a Raisin Cake Is Wrapped in Cloth

> It [the story of Christ] does not exactly work outward . . . It is rather something that surprises us from behind, from the hidden and personal part of our being . . . It is rather as if a man had found an inner room in the very heart of his own house, which he had never suspected.
>
> —G. K. Chesterton, *The Everlasting Man*

ALL DAY I PRAY until I forget to eat the little raisin cake wrapped in cloth. I pray for the lame, the crippled, and those carried on biers. I pray for the blind, the deaf, the poor, the destitute. If I hear someone crying or pleading with God, I go to them. I tell them of my hope in our God. I pray for the maimed. The leper. The possessed. When I feel the heat of the sun, I fold my headcloth over my forehead again. Someone has given me another raisin cake wrapped in a cloth. Someone has given me another walking stick. I give it to someone who needs it.

I hear a cry above the others. I find the woman, and I pray for her. She lost a child, probably taken by the herders who come into the city. Maybe one of them had a wife who had no child. Or whose child had died. "Is there no one to track them into the desert?" she pleads. I sit with her while she grieves.

I pray in the main courtyard of the temple all day. At night, I sleep with other widows in our rooms in the smaller women's courtyard off the main courtyard. I hear the soldiers passing in the street. I see the flicker of the centurions' barrel fires. I hear the noise of chariots. What would it be to ride in a chariot behind those horses that rumble the streets when they pass? But Scripture is a chariot. I wonder where that foolish thought came from. How pitiful thoughts are—forgotten little cakes wrapped in cloth. I pray for the soldiers. They have duties that keep them from God. I grieve for the world. I offer it my prayers.

Prayer is a longing for the absence of separation.

I hear the olive orchards from the hill—I hear their voices raised in praise. Once, I played there as a girl. Once, I became lost in the orchard while my mother gathered olives after dark. I sat with the small animals until my mother called. When I was older, I helped her pick the olives. I helped her press them with the mortar and pestle to make oil for our lamp.

In the daylight, I watched the men shake the olive trees, hitting the branches with poles until the olives fell. The small animals, resting in the

Uprising of Goats

shade of the trees, would run. The men left a few olives for the wayfarers. It's what Scripture instructed them to do.

After dark, I stand in the main courtyard under the moon as round as prayer. I pray when I go into the women's small courtyard to sleep. I pray in my dreams. I dream I am praying. I pray I am dreaming when I hear the noise of trouble in the streets—the crazy ones, the beggars, the robbers. Prayer is silver as an olive orchard wrapped in moonlight.

"Be quiet, Anna," someone says.

"She's dreaming again," another widow interrupts. "As if we didn't have enough worries, she stirs them up in her sleep. She invents more sorrows."

Lord, there is war in my thoughts. What must it be for others? The evil one tries to interrupt my prayers. Lord, I have seen into your heavens. Yet I cannot keep my mind there. Hosts after hosts upon hosts. Do we stand with them? Do we stand in your courtyard? In front of your throne? Will you tell us where to go? Will there be someone there to guide us when your heaven is turned upside down like fishing boats on the shore?

In the morning, I hear a little flock of goats. A man tries to lead them with a stick. I lead my prayers with my walking stick. Sometimes prayers are unruly. They bleat and make noise. I wrestle with the thoughts that are as hard to manage as goats.

Someone puts a fig in my hand. I thank them. I hold the fig up in the air. No beggar takes it. I eat the fig, giving thanks to God.

In the mornings, I hear the priests inside the temple, where women cannot go. I hear Simeon enter the courtyard from the street. Each morning, he says he will not see death before he sees the Lord's Christ, the consolation of Israel. I feel the uprising of air. I ride the chariots of praise—salvation is upon us. Blessed is the Lord of Hosts. Holy. Holy. The earth is full of holiness. You have given us your foreshadowings: you came as Melchizedek, as the messengers to Abraham, as the angel who wrestled with Jacob, as the appearance of one sitting on his throne to Isaiah, as the one walking in the furnace with Daniel's friends. What will you do now? How will you reveal yourself to us?

Lord, my thoughts wander like a flock of goats. What is death? I think sometimes I'm more dead than alive. I'm past the years of dying. Is death passing through an olive orchard with my thoughts catching on the gnarled roots, tripping me up? Or are we transformed from goats to new beings in your presence? Do we keep our ears or hooves? No, we are not goats. We are

A Chapter in Which a Raisin Cake Is Wrapped in Cloth

people that act like goats. I feel a goat tongue in my mouth. I nat and bleat. Yet you allow me to stay in your presence.

The Lord's hosts are in the corners of the courtyard. They stand like olive trees when they blossom. They are bright sunlight, but Lord, you are brighter. Grace to you and peace to your Almighty name. Forgive us, Lord. We're blind to what you are. Or we see less of you than there is to see. Surely you have borne our grief and carried our sorrows. You are wounded for our transgressions, and with your stripes, we are healed. All prophets promise your coming. Our doors are open. Our houses ready. We have not heard from you since Malachi. Our eyes will see, and we will say, "The Lord is magnified from the border of Israel" (Mal 1:5).

Long ago, my husband was sick. I went to the marketplace and when I returned, he was on the floor. I think he was trying to get to the door. His arms outstretched as if he was trying to reach something. If I had been there, I could have reached it for him. There were times I could hear his heart. He was always out of breath. My mother did not want me to marry him, but she finally agreed because he could provide for us. He was a kind husband.

Was it not the same with my father, Phanuel? He was sick and calling out, and I went to my grandmother's house because my mother didn't want me to hear. My father died while I was gone.

What if my father and husband passed through the main courtyard on their way through the Gate of Nicanor into the temple? Would they notice an old woman as someone they had known?

I stumble and fall. What had I tripped on? I don't see anything. Is it those memories cluttering the way? They should ease with age, but they live no matter how long ago they happened. No one helped me up when I fell. I was glad no one saw, or if they did, they ignored me.

Someone puts my walking stick in my hand. I thank them. It is the weight of prayer that keeps me off balance.

O God. O edge of light. O moving shadows on the wall. O roll of clouds. O birds flying there. O donkey braying in the street. O fig tree. Pomegranate. Olive orchard. Anointed olive leaves. O moving hems of the robes of widows in the open courtyard. O dust that blows there. O women sweeping in the courtyard. Little flock—your shepherd will arrive with healing in his wings.

Uprising of Goats

For years, the widows lived in a lean-to near the stables. For years, we prayed in the main courtyard of the temple and at night, returned to the lean-tos near the animals. Finally, a room with straw mattresses was opened in the women's courtyard. I didn't want to leave my place with the animals, but there were mites in the stalls. "Look at those bites on your face and arms," they said. "The soldiers drink at night as they sit by their charcoal fires. What if they try to rob you on the street when you walk from the temple in the dark?" I tell them I'm beyond danger. The soldiers know I have nothing to steal but a little raisin cake wrapped in cloth. I'm invisible to them—nothing more than a goat.

I pray until I forget the light of day is past. Sometimes I hear a voice: *Go to your room, Anna. The Lord knows you're faithful.* Where was the voice coming from? One of the priests on the way to his room? I turned, but could see no one.

Sometimes I hear voices in the streets: the animals tethered for sacrifice. The little goats know what will happen, as I know.

I pray for the weak. The suffering. I pray for God's blessings on his people. The praises pour from me. I can't hold them back. They keep coming and coming. Blessed is the Lord. The first and the last. And all that is in-between. I praise my Redeemer. The author of our lives. The coming one. You have declared it. I call it out to you.

I remember when I lined a few pebbles against my mat in the stables. I listened to their voices. I heard them praise the Lord in the night. Their little voices traveled on the wind to the olive orchard. The little stones and olive leaves tried to out-praise one another. They tried to praise as loud as the multitudes I hear from the heavens.

I am caught on earth. I am in-between this world and the next, part of one and part of the other. Lord, I feel your approach. When Simeon praises you, my own voice joins his. Are we like the stones and olive leaves? No, we are your people—hidden in every tribe. We wait for you. Are you in your chariot, your horses ready to jar our streets?

I have many prayers. Day and night cannot contain them. Sometimes I taste pomegranates when I pray. Sometimes a raisin cake. Sometimes I'm walking in an olive orchard. I see the silver underside of leaves as stars in the heavens. There is no end to praise.

AFTERWORD TO ANNA

A Chapter in Which Tenure Was Received

WHAT AM I'M DOING, if not making an uprising against silence? Why am I doing it?

I was looking at the book of Enoch online when I saw a commentator who mentioned some of the lost books, such as the Apocalypse of Noah. I thought of Noah's wife, Hispera, watching him as he wrote.

Maybe it was the afterimage of reading these biblical women whose voices were not recorded. Somehow I felt them. I would like to think it was the echo of the women's voices I felt anyway. The way the smell of rain sometimes lingers in the air after a storm.

How much *creating* can we do before we go too far?

Maybe this is about my own silence. How often I feel like I belong to a little flock of goats. I think of their feet on the mountain and hillsides, their passages over crags and rocky precipices. I am an intruder into their heights. But I can climb with them because I think that heights are found in the depths of despair. In the battering daily routine that seems to spin between a wild boredom and frantic activity. In the difficulty I had standing in front of a class. Where would I go from here? How would I do it? My introverted nature didn't seem in tune with teaching, yet it was what I did.

What is coming next? I sometimes asked. Yet I am blessed with my savior's staff leading me. Scripture says it is so.

I think this writing is a game of shadow puppets. Their substance moves behind a goat-hair bolster. I cannot see them as they are. Therefore,

Uprising of Goats

a narrative of reconstruction is dangerous as goat's feet on a steep cliff. I think of a lowly goat walking those heights. Imagination is the thread that sews the bolster. I wanted to imagine the women's voices. To hear their words settle together. They seemed alone on their cliff as they made their way across the rocks.

It was with the goats that I learned the song of the redeemed.

The president of the college called one morning. I had received tenure. I thanked him. I hung up. What would I do? Prepare for class.

My girls were back for the summer. They had found jobs. Walker had helped them.

Blessed be the Lord of my salvation.

A Chapter in Which a Group of Women See Christ's Death

There were also women looking on afar off.

—Mark 15:40

What was the song of the redeemed? The tenured in God's kingdom. How was the song to be sung? We saw the Redeemer with our eyes. Our faces swelled with tears. We watched his death on the cross. We felt the earth shake until large rocks split (Matt 27:51). We saw him carried into the tomb. We saw the stone cover the opening. We felt the darkness. At the end of the Sabbath, when it was still dark, we went to the tomb with spices to anoint his body, but there was a large stone covering the opening. We felt another earthquake. An angel descended from heaven and rolled back the stone from the door of the tomb and sat upon it (Matt 28:2). He was dressed in lightning. He said, *Jesus is not here, for he is risen*. We looked in the tomb. We saw the body was not there. How could we breathe? How could we speak? At the cross, our voices filled with grief. Now there was amazement. Now there was a wild fear of what we hoped: *Go quickly and tell his disciples that he is risen from the dead. He goes before you into Galilee. You will see him there*. We knew it then. Mary Magdalene and Joanna and Mary Clopas, the mother of James, along with other women that were among us (Luke 24:10). Joanna, the wife of Chuzas, Herod's steward. Mary Salome. Susanna. More of the unnamed. He is NOT IN THE TOMB! We bowed our faces to the ground and wept as we were grazing.

A Chapter in Which a Sabbatical and a Divorce Appear

AFTER I RECEIVED TENURE, I thought of a sabbatical. I could have taken it the year after receiving tenure, but I decided to delay it. I began to think it was a mistake. What was it about time on my own that seemed so frightening? I called the dean's office. Was it too late to apply for next year? Other voices were coming and I needed time. I knew these next voices were a group. I decided they were Philip's daughters, who prophesied in the book of Acts. What were their names? What did they say? What was prophecy?

I had waited too long, but if I could get a proposal in tomorrow . . . What could I do? Was it possible to write a proposal in a day? I supposed it was. If I got a sabbatical, I would spend next year writing the rest of the book on the voices of biblical women. I was already thinking ahead. I wanted to work on the four daughters of Philip. No, I didn't want to wait. I thought of a trip to Turkey and Caesarea. It would be a short trip. I didn't want to write there. I just wanted to see the land where these daughters had lived. I already heard their voices.

I didn't think a day wasn't enough time to write a proposal, especially when I had classes to teach. Yet I started with the explanation of what I had been doing. I had written the voices of Dorcas and Michal. I used words like "feminism" and "deconstruction of biblical text" and other words I knew the committee would like. I told the department chair I was writing a hurried proposal and would need his signature and a letter of recommendation.

Who would teach my courses next year? I would think of someone, I told him. I was overdue for a sabbatical, though we didn't get them automatically. I knew some professors who had not taken a sabbatical in many years. They wanted to be in the classroom, while my attention was elsewhere at the moment.

The department chair agreed to my application reluctantly, asking why I hadn't started on it sooner.

When I returned to the house that evening, I found the final divorce papers in the mail. I hardly had time to realize I was no longer married.

In late spring, I found that I had been granted a sabbatical for the coming academic year. I worried whether I could afford it. A sabbatical came with half-pay. I had a former mother-in-law who was ill. Her nursing home bills were eating into her assets. Soon there would be nothing left. It was possible to take it with you, after all.

Walker called and asked if I would help. He was the main provider for our daughters' college tuition. I had to give him that.

I had to abandon the four daughters of Philip as the semester went on. I had meetings to attend and papers to grade. I kept notes, but I couldn't concentrate on my project except in small pieces of time. I also searched for available grants and decided to apply to Baylor University's scholar-in-residence program because I wanted to be near their library. I wanted to go to Caesarea, where the sisters were born, and to Hierapolis in Turkey, where my research led me to believe they had died, though it was not clear.

I spent another week filling out grants, writing a prospectus for my plans. The programs were competitive. I had to make my application solid.

In time, I received a letter saying I had received a fellowship to Baylor University for their scholar-in-residence program. Then I received a sabbatical from my college, also for the fall semester, and a travel grant from a foundation to go to Caesarea and Hierapolis.

I could find no record of the names of Philip's daughters. I would have to give them names: Philipa, Clauda, Prudah, and Lucina. Those names would do as replacements. Names as though they were names. Names made to look as though they were the daughters' names, like four bolsters of goat hair.

Uprising of Goats

There was a flame in my head. The smell of smoke haunted me. I woke sometimes thinking the house was on fire. Through these voices, I had to make known that which had been. No, that which could have been.

THE PARTING

A Chapter in Which the Four Daughters of Philip Are Called by Name

AND THE NEXT DAY we that were of Paul's company departed, and came unto Caesarea; and we entered into the house of Philip, the evangelist, one of the seven, and abode with him. And the same man had four daughters, virgins, which did prophesy.

—ACTS 21:8–9

Philipa

I WRITE THIS FOR whoever picks it up. It's about my father, Philip, one of the seven chosen in the upper room. It is what he told us—what my three sisters and I decided to record. It is what we heard from different apostles and other travelers when they came to our house in Caesarea. They talked about their journeys, telling us of all they had experienced since the crucifixion. It was my sister, Clauda, who insisted we write; or rather, she started writing, and we followed. As I am the oldest, I begin.

Jesus had been with them. Then he was crucified. Then they heard he was seen after the crucifixion. He was dead. Then alive? How had he returned? They didn't understand the reversal. What had happened? They wanted to see him. Would they know him if they did? They had suffered a setback. A catastrophe. Their leader had been crucified. Their boat had lost its shore. Now he was back?

They heard Jesus was seen by Mary Magdalene and the other women at the tomb. He was seen on the road to Emmaus. He had talked to some of his apostles before they knew who he was. He continued to be seen by different people in various places after his death.

Jesus' followers grieved when he was crucified. Then they heard—he was alive! There was expectation instead of despair. They wanted to be together. The word went out: they were supposed to meet in Jerusalem. Those who left returned to Jerusalem. It also was the Feast of Weeks—a gathering to remember when God gave the Law on Mount Sinai.

After Jesus was seen, he left again. My father said that crowds moved through the streets of Jerusalem. He said he heard the different languages of the Jews who had come from everywhere for the Feast of Weeks. There was

Philipa

the clatter of camels and donkeys, the squeal of pigs and goats and sheep, the flap of pigeons, the bark of dogs. I imagined the sellers of figs and dates, of cloth and goatskins, all stopping to talk. Each day, my father walked through the crowded streets to a house near the temple. He climbed the stairs and entered a large room filled with people. This was the upper room where they met together in those confounding days after the crucifixion.

Jesus told his apostles he had to leave so the Comforter would come, a Comforter who was the Spirit of Truth. But what was this truth? Jesus said the Comforter would tell them what they needed to know. From God through Christ through the Comforter to them. The men had not understood that Jesus would leave by the cross. Sometimes they still couldn't grasp it.

I thought about what I heard when my father taught us the Scriptures. It was how we learned to read and write. We wrote, "The stone which the builders refused became the cornerstone" (Ps 118:22). Was that the truth Jesus spoke about? He would be refused? Was that what his crucifixion was? Then he would become the cornerstone? We knew that he was seen by his believers. He had talked to his apostles. He was taken from the cross, dead, and placed in a tomb. But when others arrived, his body was not there. Later, the apostles said he sat talking with them. Or when they were walking, he would join them on the road. He said they would receive power to witness in Jerusalem, in Judea and Samaria, in the corners of the earth. After he spoke to them, he departed through the clouds. Two men were there saying he would return in the same way. He would step out of heaven and back to the earth.

My father said they had to wait in Jerusalem for the promise. But what was the promise? The Holy Ghost would come. Who was this Holy Ghost? Another person like Christ? Would he be crucified too?

My father sat with the apostles in the upper room: Peter, James, John, Andrew, Thomas, Bartholomew, Matthew, Simon, James, the son of Alphaeus, and Thaddaeus (sometimes called Judas, but not the Iscariot). They continued in prayer for several days. They studied Scriptures. Sometimes they fasted. At night, they retired to their rooms. Other travelers slept on roofs or camped near the corrals on the outskirts of Jerusalem.

We asked my father if he knew how long they would wait in Jerusalem, and he said at first that they didn't know. The travelers had wanted to leave Jerusalem, but knew they had been told to wait until the Comforter came. In the meantime, Peter stood up in the room and suggested they elect another apostle, which, after the death of Judas, would make twelve of them again.

Barsabbas Justus, called Joseph, and Matthias were nominated. The lot fell to Matthias as the twelfth apostle. We asked our father to tell the story again and again.

One morning when they had gathered in the upper room, they heard the wind. The birds flew away. Was it a storm? But there were no clouds. The roar of the wind swept through the open windows. With the wind came pieces of fire. What were they? It was as if small birds hovered over their heads. But they were not birds, but something like birds made of air or light as if it were fire. The pieces of fire were split as the hooves of sheep are split, but this split was of air or fire, which sat upon each head. My father told us how everyone spoke as the cloven fire hovered above them. Everyone spoke in another language. What were they saying? They didn't know. But it was praise to our God. Others said they could understand the language, if it was from the place they were from. It was as if all languages came together in the room and interchanged. People who didn't know a certain language could speak it, while others to whom the language belonged could understand. The ones speaking didn't know what they were saying. The words joined anyone who would speak what came from their mouth: not a learned language, but words spoken suddenly without understanding except by someone else. They didn't know what they were saying, but they heard the others say they recognized the languages each was speaking. The Tower of Babel had separated the people with languages. But this strange language, or languages, brought them together. People from Galilee, Parthia, Mede, Elam, Mesopotamia, Judea, Cappadocia, Pontus, Asia, Phrygia, Pamphylia, Egypt, Libya, Cyrene, Rome, Crete, Arabia, said, "How can we speak what others understand, but we, ourselves, cannot? How can people speak another language they didn't learn?"

After Babel, the people could not understand one another. They could understand their own kind, but not others. Now the people spoke and didn't know what they were speaking, but it brought them together instead of separating them.

My father was amazed I put all he said onto the papyrus. But as he spoke, I could image what it could have been like in Jerusalem. We had to remind ourselves we were in our house in Caesarea and not Jerusalem.

My father said that Peter had stood in the upper room and told how the prophet Joel had said God would pour out his spirit. "Your daughters

Philipa

will prophesy—Joel 2:28," Peter said. "Your sons too." But it was *daughters* that my sisters, Clauda, Prudah, Lucina, and I heard.

Now we heard that Peter, one of the apostles, was coming to Caesarea. Cornelius, the centurion, had called him from Joppa.

When Peter arrived, he prayed for us to receive the Holy Spirit. I wanted to cry. I wanted to run. I stammered and was embarrassed. I stammered again. I felt the rush of strange words from my mouth. I could hear my voice speaking a language I didn't know. I could not understand, but I heard my voice speaking as though I did. My sisters and I were filled with the Holy Spirit when Peter came into our meeting in Caesarea. My mother would not open her mouth. She looked at us in bewilderment. This was prophecy? To me, it was flying with the birds. I was above the meeting. Above Caesarea.

It was as if we were babbling children. My sisters and I had played the Tower of Babel in Caesarea, each going to our own corner of the room and speaking differently from one another. We had played David and Goliath. I, Philipa, was clothed in goatskins as Goliath because I was the oldest.

When we were girls, my sisters and I tried to catch birds. We spread grain on the ground. Then we would lie flat and motionless with the grain by our outstretched hands. But when the sparrows came close to eat, sometimes nearly brushing our hands, we only watched them peck the grain— we didn't want to catch them. They were so unsure, as if they would have nothing to eat unless they picked up the grain as quickly as they could. But this was not play. It was a parting from what we knew.

"Your daughters will prophesy." What would we say? The men put their hands on our heads and prayed in our meeting in Caesarea. We would see into heaven and earth. We would see blood, fire, and smoke. The sun would turn to darkness and the moon into blood before Jesus came again.

After Peter left, we met in our houses in Caesarea. We continued in prayer sometimes for days. My sisters and I made lentil cakes and served them with pomegranates and figs and dates. We heard what was happening— thousands were being converted in Jerusalem, baptized by the tongues of fire. The conversions continued in Caesarea. Travelers told us what was happening in other places as well.

Uprising of Goats

> For a while in Jerusalem, there had been talk of staying together in a group. For a while, the believers sold all they had and shared everything in common.

My father continued to tell us of the days in the upper room in Jerusalem. He was one of seven men chosen to care for the widows, the helpless. The other disciples were Stephen, Prochorus, Nicanor, Timon, Parmenas, and Nicolas. We wrote down our father's words. Sometimes he spelled the names for us. We had to record them. It was part of the prophecies also. All of us wrote. It was amazing. We heard the same stories and lived through the same events, but we each interpreted them in our own way.

All the disciples went about their work. Stephen, especially, got in trouble with everyone—with the Libertines, the Cyrenians, the Alexandrians, and those in Cilicia and Asia. You'd think healing the lame and casting out demons would matter, but no. Stephen touched the broken hearts and stroked them as though they were wounded sparrows in his hand. My sisters and I imagined the widows our father and the other disciples helped. The widows came into the room silent. They left sounding like a courtyard full of birds.

With my father, we visited the fatherless and the widows in Caesarea and the nearby towns. I often felt my father's restlessness. I wondered if he was thinking of the travels he had made before he came to Caesarea and had us. I was afraid we kept him in one place when he wanted to travel. But he stayed with us, except for the necessary trips for evangelism.

We played with the children in the street. "The conies are feeble but they make their houses in the rock" (Prov 31:26). My sisters and I played Scripture games with the children.

Tychias, Marcus, and Justins tossed stones at us, skipping them at our feet until the children were afraid of them. We took up the stones and played with them. We washed a dove's crate and put the stones in it, two by two. We made a Noah's ark that the children lifted in their hands. Prudah and Lucina were clouds and thunder. Clauda and I were the flood.

We healed the rocks when they were sick or lame. Sometimes they couldn't walk. We lowered the rocks on strings into the dove's crate, just as we heard the disciples had lowered the sick on mats down from the roof into a room where Jesus was. We prayed for their healing. We covered the

Philipa

children's eyes so they would know how Bartimaeus, the blind man, felt. We helped them climb the fig tree and sycamore.

My father continued with the story of Stephen, one of the disciples, telling how he worked miracles until some in the synagogue grew tired of him. They paid men to say they heard Stephen speak blasphemy against God. Stephen's enemies continued to stir up the people.

"Run!" I would have told him if I was there.

But they caught Stephen, brought him to council, and set up false witnesses. They took him to the streets and stoned him. But Stephen looked at the sky and said, "I see God and Jesus standing on his right hand" (Acts 7:55).

After Stephen's burial, the six disciples scattered, leaving behind their idea of staying together.

My father was told to go to Samaria, to Gaza, Azotus, and finally, he came to Caesarea.

Each time my father told us about Stephen, we cried. After a while, we emptied the dove cage of stones and did not play our game with the children again.

Being filled with the Holy Spirit began with a willingness to speak. Sometimes I held the words to myself, thinking they didn't matter. Other times I said what I thought. Interpretation followed the prophecy. If I spoke in tongues, someone interpreted what I said, usually one of my sisters. What if it was not true? What if our words didn't match? What if my sisters made up the interpretation? What if I made up the language I didn't know?

I heard the strange words in my mouth. They came first in a language I didn't know. Then I heard Lucina's voice interpreting my strange words in our own language: "You do not know who I am. You do not know when I will speak. Or what I will say. Or how I will work. You do not know me. But I am among you when you do not know it. I speak what I speak. Listen to what I say. Obey my words. I will speak what you don't expect. I will tell you of my ways."

I felt the expectation in the meetings in our house and in the house of the centurion. I wanted to hear the strange and unknown words that came from my mouth as they worked their way from silence. There was a purpose for words. Words were all we had to tell the story of Jesus. Words defeated silence. That's what was holy about them.

Uprising of Goats

We heard of the persecutions. Friends asked us not to talk of our faith. They stopped coming to our house. Finally, they laughed at us. Would they tell others? Would soldiers come to our house? The four of us could be our own friends—we always were together. I could hardly tell myself from my sisters, or my dress from their dresses.

We walked to meetings in the centurion's house, with the calls of the blind and the beggars echoing in the narrow streets. Maybe we would have new friends. At every meeting there were more people.

I had a prophecy that addressed our fears: "I have given you the sword that cuts through the darkness that wraps the world. I have put the light in your hands. I am the lion of the tribe of Judah and I roar for you."

Each meeting, these prophecies came. Jesus had not left us alone on the earth. He was with us, even to the end of our world.

After those early days in Jerusalem, Philip, my father, went to Samaria and preached Christ. The people listened to what my father said and saw the miracles he did. Unclean spirits, crying with a loud voice, came out of many who were possessed by them, while many struck with palsies and lameness were healed. But there was a man, Simon Magnus, who used sorcery on the people of Samaria, telling them it was the power of God. But when Magnus heard my father preaching about God and Jesus Christ, he believed and was baptized. Philip, my father, was amazed at the miracles and signs that were performed. Now, when the apostles in Jerusalem heard that Samaria had received the word of God, they sent Peter and John.

"Have they received the Holy Ghost?" the apostles asked.

"No," my father said. "They've only been baptized in the name of Jesus."

The apostles prayed for them and laid hands upon them, and they received the Holy Ghost.

Afterwards, my father returned to Jerusalem with Peter and John, stopping to preach the gospel in many villages in Samaria.

Then my father went into the desert on a road from Jerusalem toward Gaza, where he baptized a man, and thereafter, was caught up by the Spirit and flew away. Later, he was found in Azotus.

My father, the flying man.

"How did you disappear from the desert?" Prudah asked.

"I just did," he said. "The desert suddenly changed into a town."

Philipa

Paul and his company came to Caesarea to stay for many days. Paul, who had caused havoc in the church until he was converted—Paul, now called an apostle—Paul, the sudden one—was among us. I felt myself tremble as he approached. I saw my father's fear also. This was Paul, who had been at the stoning of Stephen. Paul, who consented to the stoning. This was Paul, who had seen Christians beaten, who had himself suffered beatings and scourgings after he became a Christian.

Maybe Christianity was a parting from what he expected.

Why had our father welcomed Paul? Was it palsy Paul had? Or was it his energy for Christ, all bound up in one man? Sometimes he stumbled over his clothes and goatskins, and his words as well. Often his eyes squinted as though he had trouble seeing. What was wrong with this man? Yet we felt the power that surrounded him. I saw Paul was a man, not as large as he seemed at first. He was not the man we heard he was. His arrival was a parting from what we had thought.

In the meetings, Lucina pulled her headcloth over her face to hide from Paul. Prudah kept nudging her to behave. When we returned from a meeting at the house of Cornelius, the centurion, we told our mother that Paul was going to stay at our house! She went to her room again and didn't come out until the next day.

Travelers brought news from different places while Paul was at our house. Believers were making a feast of communion. Believers were misinterpreting salvation. Believers were flying everywhere, doing whatever seemed right to them. Paul was a learned man. He reasoned with the new believers. He provided thought and logic. He preached his way "through the waters" (Isa 43:2; Ezek 47:4), bringing Christianity into harbor. He wrote how faith should take shape. He imposed order. He gave process. But where was the spirit, the heart, the air?

We listened to the men argue. We were overshadowed by Paul. He talked. He wrote. We served. We copied. Did he recognize our prophecy? Was he afraid we would become like the sea when the wind swept it? Philip, our father, was our harbor. Christ, our Lord, was our harbor.

Did they know we could write about them? Did they know we could also write what we thought? But could we write like them—with their thoughts? Our father, Philip, taught us to write. But Paul had been educated. We felt the power of his mind and felt small before him.

Paul liked the word "law." What did it mean to have the law of Christ?

Uprising of Goats

We listened to Paul's understanding of Christ's advent on earth. We listened as we prepared meals. We listened as we sat in the room with him. We were justified by Christ's faithfulness to death. It was Christ's faithfulness, not our faithfulness. What was the law in the Scriptures, the writings? There had been Abraham's covenant. Noah's covenant. Now there was the law of Christ: we should love one another. I did not feel love from Paul. Judgment, rather, and caution. Faith was our righteousness. But there were obligations. The sovereignty of God was law. Or was it the law of God's sovereignty? Why had the law been given? The law we couldn't keep? The law revealed sin. The law showed us how to please God. But we could not keep the law. Even if we could, the law was powerless to save us, as was the sacrifice of animals.

The children begged us to play with them. Prudah was restless and ran with them on the street.

While Paul and his company were in Caesarea, in the middle of their arguments, a prophet named Agabus came from Judea. He took Paul's girdle and bound his hands and feet and said that the Jews at Jerusalem would bind him and deliver him into the hands of the Gentiles.

But Paul answered that he was ready not only to be bound, but to die in Jerusalem for the name of the Lord Jesus, and he prepared to leave. Maybe Paul was the twelfth apostle, rather than Matthias, the one elected by men. Maybe he was the Gentile apostle. The one who set believers straight.

In a few days, Paul and his company left for Jerusalem with some of our men from Caesarea. I knew our father longed to go, but he stayed with our mother, who was ill.

Later that afternoon, when they were gone and we had fewer meals to prepare, we played miracles. We turned a stone into a fish. We healed sick birds. We bound one another's hands.

My mother feared for my father's life. Often, we heard them talk. Sometimes we heard them disagree. Sometimes she despaired. But we had courage. If Philip, our father, was killed—if we were killed for our faith, we would see God. Had not Stephen said, "I see the heavens opened, and the Son of Man standing on the right hand of God?" (Acts 7:56).

When Jesus comes again, he won't be wearing a crown of thorns. He won't be riding on a donkey. He won't be seeing another crooked night. He

Philipa

won't be going to the cross. We knew it would be soon. Hadn't Christ said this generation would not pass?

The road was warm under our feet. We walked through the dust as we went to the aqueduct where water flowed from the spring near Mount Carmel. We saw the straight line of the horizon across the sea. We listened to the waves. We felt the constant wind flapping our tunics. We watched the fishermen hang their nets of fish along the wall.

We walked to the public fountains for water. We saw the pigeons and doves flapping in their cages. The sheepfolds. The camels. Donkeys. Pigs squealing. We shopped in the marketplace and washed the lentils we bought. We helped our mother cook, though more often now it was we who prepared the meals while she watched.

Often, the meetings were at our house. Other times, we walked behind our father to the meetings in other houses, usually to the home of Cornelius, the centurion. Sometimes our troubled mother walked with us. Sometimes she stayed at our house.

"The rising moon is in the sycamore," Clauda said.

We looked at the moon in the top of the tree that pointed to the stars, those insects of the night.

"The moon comes to visit," Lucina said.

I thought it looked like a millstone for grinding the grain.

We watched the moon until it stepped further into the black puddle of the night.

"We should build a fire to keep the moon warm," Prudah said. "That's why it leaves."

It's what stays with me—the sun will turn to dark and the moon to blood before his return.

"The stars are the birds of heaven," I told my sisters as we stood on the roof of our house that night. As I worked with my sisters in the days that followed, I felt the wings that flew through our writing. We had been given faith. We had been given a gift we had to struggle with. It was small as a seed that grows into a tree—the birds make their nests in its shade.

Clauda

OUR MEETINGS WERE WILD with prophecy. After the Apostle Peter came to Caesarea and baptized us in the Holy Spirit, we couldn't stop prophesying. We heard that in Joppa, Peter raised a seamstress from the dead. He upset everything we knew. We heard the shrieks of the departing spirits that did not belong. He said he had a vision on his way to Caesarea. He could come to us, even us.

There were rumors of persecutions. Fear was a wildfire. People were leaving for other countries—or they were driven away. Everyone spoke until we didn't know one prophecy from another. The words were a jumble we were left to sort.

"And by the sea, the sea will take . . ." It was the beginning of another prophecy in the meeting. I stopped and would say nothing more because I could feel the end of it coming. I didn't want us to be among the believers dispersed to far places, though the resurrected Christ led us. If we left Caesarea, that is, which we would not. Unless we received the word to go. Unless it were prophesized. Then we who had never stepped on the water would go on a ship to another place. Asia, I suppose. We heard of the believers there. We knew some who went. We might be needed there. Our mother would not go, could not go. We heard it too much. Darkness and water already there. What did they speak in Asia, this being after Babel? We named our fears as Adam named the animals that clothed him, each a reminder of our need.

"It is he who sits on the circle of the earth" (Isa 40:22). Look at his round sky. It is he who brings out the host of stars and calls them by name.

Clauda

Sometimes my sisters and I sat among the stone anchors by the sea, imagining Jesus walking to us across the water. Sometimes I watched Prudah and Lucina collect shells. The shore was full of them. They were crushed to pave the streets of Caesarea. They were tossed by children.

We watched ships come into the breakwaters built out into the sea. We stood on the stone walls of the harbor. We talked on the sand. We lived in the city built by Herod the Great. Governors and magistrates walked with pomp through the streets or were carried in their litters, surrounded by servants and guards.

Our father continued to tell us of the days in Jerusalem when the Comforter came. They hadn't expected Jesus would leave by the cross. Sometimes they still seemed amazed. It was as if it was a new thought, returning again and again. Sometimes, when my father was working, I would see a certain look on his face and know he was remembering that Christ had been crucified and that his followers were looking for direction. Think of it: What if what Christ had said was a lie? He had been the leader. He turned the world upside down. Given men a new way to think. He was the way, the truth, the life. Then he was dead! What had happened? They knew later. God had to judge sin. He did so by placing all of humanity's sins upon Jesus and putting him to death. Sin died on the cross. All we had to do was accept it. The cross was the depository for God's anger. Then Christ was resurrected, and we with him, if we also believed. We knew it by prophecy. We knew it by our truth.

I remembered what I'd heard about the crucifixion and wrote it down. Maybe it was why my father had taught us to write. Maybe it was why I wanted to write. To preserve what had happened. I liked writing the words, whatever it was they said.

Some of the women came to Jesus' tomb with spices.

"But they knew the tomb was shut," Prudah said.

"Yes, but that's what they did—Mary Magdalene, Joanna, Susanna, and the others."

There had been an earthquake at the tomb, after which an angel descended from heaven and rolled back the stone. The women said it was an angel with a face like lightning. The angel told them not to be afraid. Jesus, who was crucified, was not there, but had risen. The angel told the women to go and tell Jesus' apostles.

"All hail," the angel said. I wrote that down and looked at the words: "All hail."

The women fled the tomb, and he was standing before them on the road. Mary reached for him, but he asked her not to hold him.

I would have held him by the feet also to keep him on earth.

I tried to write down everyone who had seen him. Mary Magdalene and the women, James, the son of Mary and Joseph, and on several occasions Jesus' other disciples.

I thought of all the prophesying, all the noise in the upper room. There always had been prophecy in the Scriptures. The Spirit of God had come upon the messengers of Saul, and they prophesied also. Even Saul lay down all day and night (1 Sam 19:24).

After the crucifixion, Jesus was taken to Joseph of Arimathaea's tomb. Nicodemus brought linen and spices to wrap him. And afterwards, they rolled a stone across the door.

The next morning, Mary Magdalene brought spices. How did she think she would move the stone? Didn't the women think?

I wrote what I heard had happened. Weren't the events in the Scriptures written? Wasn't the book still being written? Didn't God himself have a book in which he wrote our names? We needed to write about Jesus' life to preserve it, to document it. Paul was here writing. Peter was preaching and keeping notes. The disciples visited our house in Caesarea. We sat with them, listening. All of us wrote about the events we heard or experienced. This writing colony.

How could we do it?

For precept must be upon precept, line upon line, here a little and there a little.

Sometimes when I slept, I thought I saw a bright light.

I kept writing about what Philip, our father, did. His travels and miracles. I wanted to know more about the miracles, but my father would not talk much of them. It was the ordinary. It was salvation. It was faith that was more important.

Paul was writing. We stood in awe of him when he came to our house in Caesarea. Sometimes another apostle, Luke, was with him, who ministered to our mother. Sometimes others were with him. We saw Paul bent over his papyrus with his stylus, his inkwell on our table. Sometimes we made copies of his letters.

Clauda

But what about history since Malachi? What came before Paul's letters? Where were the life and sayings of Christ?

We sat around the oil lamp and listened to my father talk to Paul and his companions. All around us, the house was dark, shadowed like the darkness of the past if we didn't write it—record it.

We wrote about our father's travels. We wrote about the upper room in Jerusalem. For a while we started from the crucifixion backward. Then we worked forward in his life. Later, we added events from the middle of Christ's life. At other times, we worked on Christ's genealogy. We wrote the sayings of Jesus. He spoke in Aramaic. We wrote in Greek. Where was the overall story of his life? We were writing fragments, plodding like camels. We lived in Caesarea by the sea, but we were camels walking in the desert with four hooves, the sand sometimes covering the tracks we made. How would the fragments be tied together? But were the comets tied together as they walked the sky?

Philipa prophesied about our father in a meeting one night: "Long will be the way ahead of you—many shall be your places."

We always listened to Philipa. She listened to the Scriptures the men read. Then there was another prophecy in the meeting, this one by Lucina. Philipa, who usually gave the message in tongues, interpreted the message: "I see a marketplace with cages of birds. In some cages there is one bird. In other cages, there are several. I am working on the smallest part of the cage: the latch on the door—so when the door closes, it will not stay shut. Sometimes there is a cage inside a cage. I dismantle the hinges, the walls, the floor, the roof. I dismantle all. You are free to fly into the air."

We knew Jesus had ascended. He had gone from earth. But we would see him again. He must be in heaven now, because the Comforter had come. Maybe the message meant we could fly there to be with him. He was gone and we were alone. How could I feel alone when I had my parents and sisters and a houseful of believers at meeting? Why were we left desolate without a savior? How could he leave us with the Holy Ghost, who was like the air? In Caesarea, we were unsure, stumbling, awkward, uncertain of our way until we prayed and felt renewed. We believed Jesus was coming back to get Rome off our backs. To transform the world (Matt 24:34; Luke 21:32).

He brought his people to the border of his sanctuary. "Even to this mountain, which his right hand had purchased" (Ps 78:54). His right hand was Christ, the camel who carried us. "Remember your congregation, which you purchased of old" (Ps 74:2).

Jesus, the salvation of Jehovah. Jesus, the camel who carried our burdens.

Prophecy was more than speaking in tongues. It was speaking truth. Many women had been prophets: Deborah, Noadiah, even Huldah.

Elizabeth, the mother of John the Baptist, was filled with the Holy Spirit. When she saw Mary, she told her she would be the mother of Christ. Prophecy spoke truth. Yes, to prophesy was to speak truth. It provided direction for our meetings. We knew what to pray for. We knew how to make war against our despondency, our disheartedness, our weakness. Prophecy let us know that God was with us. It provided comfort. It caused us to praise. It confirmed what we read in the Scriptures. It showed us the way.

To prophesy was like riding a young camel—wobbly, just learning to travel.

Miriam, the sister of Moses, had been a prophetess. Miriam was also an unmarried woman, a virgin, who prophesied. She also bore reproach because she spoke against Moses, who had married an Ethiopian. We bore reproach because we were unmarried. We saw girls we knew with their husbands and babies.

"We don't have a brother to speak against."

"We have sisters."

"What if I marry an Ethiopian? What would you say?"

"At least one of us has a husband."

"Our husband is Christ."

Sometimes Prudah cried when we read from the Scriptures. She had dark prophecies and visions. There was a time coming when there would be fire and smoke. It was a time yet ahead for the world. Sometimes she trembled as she prophesied, fearing God. But Jesus ministered to us as he had ministered to Mary Magdalene; Joanna, the wife of Herod's steward; Mary, the mother of James; Susanna; Salome; and the others. He ministered to us as though he were alive there with us. We prayed, and we cried as we prayed. Afterwards, we were strengthened in our bafflement.

"Were any of his apostles women?" Lucina asked.

"Were any of his disciples women?" Philipa asked.

Clauda

"Wasn't it our father who was chosen in the upper room to serve the old women?" I reminded them. "'Let this sink down into your ears.'" I told them, quoting Luke 9:44.

We wrote what we heard about Jesus. At night we read what we had written.

The people he sent out came back saying, "Even the demons are subject to us through your name." But more important than subjecting spirits to their command was that their names were written in a book in heaven (Luke 10:19–20).

Moses knew it too. He had asked forgiveness for the sins of his people so their names would not be blotted out of the book the Lord had written (Exod 32:32).

"God sits in heaven writing names in a book?" Prudah asked.

"Apparently," Philipa answered.

I felt the camels that caravanned through our writing.

We had letters from believers at Ephesus, Sardis, Pergamum, Hierapolis, and other churches in Asia. We read of their struggles in our meeting. Those people running everywhere—those new believers, unruly as young camels in the corral. I knew my father longed to travel, but we held him back. Sometimes we longed to travel also, but we were women.

"Do you think we'll be called from Caesarea?" Lucina asked. Philipa said no, but at night I heard her troubled dreams. Did the sea, which had been a closed door, give an indication it might open?

Later, we *would* sail from the harbor at Caesarea, carrying our family history with its unknown parts, its murky and different versions of possibilities. Not a hoof left behind (Exod 10:26). I felt it in a dream, but didn't tell my mother or sisters.

A few of us—my family and a few other believers—prayed in the dim room of our house at dusk. We could feel the Holy Spirit, the Comforter, in the room with us. We worshipped God. Nothing mattered but his presence. Nothing mattered but the assurance that he was with us. A withered hand, a withered heart. Desperation. Hopelessness. Fear. Compromise. We felt our husband, Christ. We felt the fellowship of believers. There were times we prayed, and it seemed the room was lifted on a camel's back. Our burdens were carried. We knit into one group. We prayed for the apostasy that ran in the new churches like seawater. Believers were being deceived. Ever learning, never able to come to the truth.

Uprising of Goats

We feared the soldiers. We could be taken to prison. Sent from our homes. We were the moon trailing the earth as if we were a camel on a rope. Yet we were not alone. We remembered the names Paul prayed for: Marcus, Barnabas, Justus, Epaphras, Demas, Archippus, Timothy, and the church at Nymphas' house in Laodicea. And for them in Hierapolis (Col 4:13).

We prayed for the tide that seemed to be against us. We longed for the return of Christ. Why did he tarry? We felt the dark powers over us. We knew others felt them too. We rowed against the waves. We prayed for mercy. We prayed for strength. We read Scriptures. God's words lived in those Scriptures. His power was transferred to us. His power was unloaded for us like cargo from the ships that came into port.

I would like to be holy. I would like to say I felt his presence at all time, but there were the times when Prudah howled and Lucina cried and our mother ranted. Why had we come to Christ? What had it been but trouble and separation from others? How could we believe in the unseen when the seen was before us every night and day in horror. We were outcasts. We went to the market two by two, with one pair of sisters always staying in the house with our mother. It always was with relief when we saw our sisters return or when we ourselves returned to the house. How did our father know the truth he proclaimed? How could we feel differently than him? He would pray over us. There were times we were a disappointment to him. There were times I could reach into heaven and feel nothing. What if ships came into port and their cargo holds were empty? But we would pray together with our father over us like a sail, and for a while we caught hope again and could walk in the marketplace without fear. Then another letter would come to tell of persecutions and beatings. Would we be beaten openly?

> A LETTER TO THE CAESAREANS: GREETINGS TO CORNELIUS AND THE FAITHFUL IN HIS HOUSE. GREETINGS TO PHILIP, TO HERDA, AND THE DAUGHTERS. TO OTHERS IN FAITH AND THOSE IN THEIR HOUSES. FOR ALL THOSE IN THE CHURCH AT CAESAREA, GREETINGS AND BLESSINGS IN THE NAME OF OUR LORD.

I could see Paul's writing from where I sat as my father read the letter in our meeting:

"PAUL UNTO THOSE AT CAESAREA FROM EPHESUS: I REMAINED IN ASIA WHEN TIMOTHY AND ERASTUS LEFT FOR MACEDONIA."

He planned to go with them, but determined in the spirit that there was still work to be done there.

Clauda

"Be strong."

He said he had known persecution, "In the beginning the disciples themselves ran from me. I would have been stoned by the very believers in Jerusalem if Barnabus had not persuaded them of my conversion."

Once Paul had been let down from a window in a basket. On his first visit to Caesarea, he was running from Jerusalem.

I saw Philipa cry as we read Paul's letter. She was the solid one. Prudah and Lucina could cry in an instant, and I ignored them, but when Philipa cried, I paid attention. What would become of us? Would we be tortured? Would we know hunger? Would we be separated from one another?

Sometimes our mother would not go to the meetings. At times, she kept Lucina with her, but the three of us went with our father.

Cornelius, the centurion, visited my mother and asked her to come to his house for church meetings, but my mother would not go.

Think of the travelers who passed Jesus on the road to Emmaus and did not know it was he who was expounding history to his believers. I couldn't remember which sister said that in church. It seemed to me we were one. Yet we saw and spoke differently.

Often travelers stayed in our house. We served them. Paul the apostle came several more times. In the end, he was with us for two years. I think we always were afraid of him. He went from city to city. Did he just get on a boat and go there? Did he follow the military roads? Did he know someone who let him stay with them, just as he stayed with us and with others in Caesarea? How was it possible to go someplace he was not from? Was it because he was a man? Was it because he was not a woman?

"I have called you into the rolling of my Spirit across the land." So went a prophecy given in our meeting. It came from Prudah. I felt a dread cross me. I wanted never to leave Caesarea. I would not leave Caesarea. Yet, I felt the sea open.

Christianity was our land, our Caesarea, with its harbor from the sea. Its constants: the wind blowing landward, the tossing waves, the children in the dusty streets. Sometimes we walked by the water to get away from the crowds at our house. The sound of the sea stilled everything. Prudah and Lucina loved the sea, but it was less to me, and to Philipa also, I think. What was the sea? Could anyone tell what it was? It was not land. It was as changing as what we understood of Christ. It was our understanding unfolding to understanding. The sea had its own mind. It was a prophecy. It was a living thing. We walked beside it, the wind tossing us, but we could not know what it was thinking, though it seemed to have a voice. Who would interpret its language? Or languages? Did it hear us? I don't think so, though it had ears, and though it wrote its stories on the shore. Yet we sat by the sea and listened. Or watched. Jesus had said he would push back the clouds, step onto the rim of the earth, and call us to him. We would fly from the earth. We would rise as camels with wings.

A Chapter in Which There Is Fellowship

Surrounding the Brazos House in Waco, Texas, where I lived during my Baylor fellowship, was Columbus Street Baptist Church, Saint Mary's Catholic Church, Central Presbyterian, Austin Street Methodist, and the Mighty Wind Worship Center. All the steeples chimed incongruently on the hour while, in the yard of the Brazos House, four male cats copulated with a small female cat for two days. I called to her, tried to reach her, to offer her sanctuary, but she would not come. The terror of the wilderness was not as terrifying as the sanctuary. I would have her spayed. She could live with me forever. But she was wild. This was the world we lived in. A place of polarities, of cruelty and mercy, of darkness and light. The Bible was a place like that. To some, the Gospel of Christ was more terrifying than the horrors of the world.

One afternoon I came into the yard of the Brazos House to find that the housekeeper had thrown out some bread for them. The cats were eating bread!

Jesus was in the wilderness with the beasts during his temptation. What kind of beasts? Mountain lions, leopards, badgers, camels, wolves, bears? Did he hear their howls and cries? Did he fear? Did they fear him? Often the demons were terrified. *Leave us alone*, they pleaded when Christ came near.

In the parking lot of the Austin Street Baptist Church was a small trailer with "Troop 412" written on it. Next to it, there were lodge poles on a flat trailer for scouting trips into went to the wilderness with the beasts.

They had to know the beasts were there. Waiting. To tear limb from limb, their bloody mouths full of gratefulness and praise. I was beginning to have visions of them. I picked up their words from the cats, those footnotes of the larger ones.

I had been stung by the pain and anger and the unfairness of it all. Others didn't seem to have my concerns. But I could never quite hit that air. I could not get clear of the large hive I was trying to place in my past. I had to spend all my energy beating my wings, gathering pollen of a kind I had not yet seen, but only hoped was there.

I felt the sting of my solitary days. Maybe they were unintentional stings, but they were stings nonetheless. I had e-mails from my daughters, and a few colleagues. Sometimes a former student needed a letter of recommendation for grad school. But mainly, I had time to work.

As I listened to the voices, I could hear the buzz of bees around the old hive that was my family. It was a large hive that flanked the small hive I had made for myself.

I tried to save stray cats when I was a child. I would feed them with scraps from our meager table, but I would find them dead by the side of the road, hit by a car passing in the night.

Prudah

I WAS ANOTHER CHANCE for my father to have a son. But no, I turned out to be a girl, just like Philipa, Clauda, and later, Lucina. Sometimes I looked at him to see if he showed disappointment.

I read the Scriptures: Zelophehad had daughters. Zelophehad, the son of Hepher, the son of Gilead, the son of Machir, the son of Manasseh, had no sons, but daughters. These are the names of his daughters: Mahlah, Noah, Hoglah, Milcah, and Tirzah.

And the daughters stood by the door of the tabernacle of the congregation. They stood before Moses, and before Eleazar, the priest, and before the princes and all the congregation, saying, "Our father died in the wilderness, and he had no sons. Why should the name of our father be done away from among his family because he has no son? Give unto us therefore a possession among the brethren of our father" (Num 27:4).

And Moses brought their cause before the Lord. And the Lord spoke to Moses, saying, "The daughters of Zelophehad speak right; give them an inheritance among their father's brethren."

If a man die, and have no son, then you shall cause his inheritance to pass
to his daughters.

—NUM 27:28

I read about other women: Tamar, Rahab, Ruth, Bathsheba.
I read that Ephraim's daughter, Sheerah, built Lower and Upper Bethhoran and Uzzen-Sheerah (1 Chron 7:24).

Uprising of Goats

>Job named his daughters Jemima, Kezia, and Karenhappach, but he also had sons.
>
>Rehoboam had sixty daughters (2 Chron 11:23).

>And these were the sons of the father of Etam: Jezreel, and Ishma, and Idbash; and the name of their sister was Hazzelelponi.
>
>—1 Chron 4:3

>And God gave to Heman fourteen sons and three daughters.
>
>—1 Chron 25:5

If my older sisters had been boys, I would have been more welcomed. I was the parting of my father's hope for a son.

There was a potter by the sea.

I watched him make his tankards and water jars, his lidded stoneware bowls and platters. I liked the storage jars in their shapes. I liked the potter's wares. His pigeon bottles. Inkwell. A fig box with a lid. A jar the shape of light on the roof. An ox figurine pitcher. Fish plates. One jar with handles too small for fingers; they were for cords to hang them on the wall.

My sisters and I walked in the marketplace. We saw the crowds of people, their talk looped like a rope over their lives.

I watched my father, Philip, talk to them the way I looked at water poured from jars carried on donkeys, or water carried on the heads of women from the aqueduct and public fountains.

The sea was water, but I thought it seemed more like fire. The Holy Spirit was water and fire. Jesus was water and fire. He was the jar poured over our heads. Out of the fire and the water, our voices spoke.

We passed the merchants. They did not notice us. Maybe it was because we were women; maybe it was because we were covered.

We walked in the marketplace without husbands. We looked at the fish scrapers and mat creasers. We looked at the curved knives with handles that looked like tongues. We smelled the fish from the sea.

Prudah

We looked at the figs, dates, grapes, pomegranates, fruits, olive oil, wheat, barley, lamb, beef, offal, and of course, fish. We walked through the bright, pungent, bloody marketplace.

What was a woman without children? A potter's jug that sits empty.

I felt despair while Philipa read Scripture to us: "Though the fig tree shall not blossom, neither shall fruit be in the vines, though the labor of the olive fail, and the fields yield no food; though the flock be cut off from the fold, and there be no herd in the stalls; Yet will I rejoice in the Lord, I will joy in the God of my salvation" (Hab 3:17–18).

Though a man doesn't ask to marry me—though the potter's hands never touch me . . .

If a prophet spoke a word that did not come true, he could be stoned. That's what bothers me about prophecy. But we did not stop.

Philipa made a prophecy in church: "We are riding the whirlwind. We are the dust of its wake. We are in the tailwind, the nightmares of the storm. We are the waterspout. We ride the turbulent waves, rolling in the tumbling waves, waiting to be pulled to heaven."

The Apostle Paul looked at her. Silence equals women.

Paul thought we should not marry. Time was short. Jesus would return at any time. We should concentrate on the Lord's work and not on husbands, though our bodies called for them. We should give our lives to Christ, though our bodies wanted children. But we had the Lord's work. We should be satisfied as we were.

Who was he to decide our lives?

"I saw Prudah watch the potter," Lucina said.

"You're the one who watches the potter," Philipa said.

"I've seen Philipa watch the men who make roof tiles," I said.

"There's a father and his three sons by the market," Clauda added. "I've watched them too."

"They will have wives. None of them will be us."

Philipa said that writing was like little birds flying. A flock of birds flying of an evening, changing formation in flight.

Clauda felt the camels plodding through each letter she wrote.

Uprising of Goats

Lucina heard the wild beasts, the fish and waves in the wilderness of the sea.

I felt the fire.

Paul sent his letters everywhere. Sometimes he asked us to copy his letters. He liked the clear, fragile hand of our writing, our mission to preserve. I think he preferred Clauda's writing.

All the words written together were like the constant breeze off the sea.

"Why are we all writing?" Philipa always asked. "Jesus didn't write."

"Except on the ground."[1] Clauda reminded her.

"He didn't leave tablets like Moses did," Philipa told her.

"In the Gospels, we have the same story in four versions." I said.

"I don't like writing," Lucina said. "I'd rather hear the voices."

"I would rather have it written. Then it is captured. Like a bird in a cage," Philipa said.

Jesus' sayings had to be absorbed into a story so that it sounded like our father, Philip, talking. We can't just have his sayings. What was he doing while he was talking, while he was teaching?

We wrote down what we remembered, or what we heard. We wrote sometimes as we cooked, splotting the parchment with our damp hands. We heard many versions from the travelers. Some of the stories were similar, and we decided it was the same story. But whose version should we write?

We couldn't agree, so we each wrote in our own way.

How did we know what to write? How did we know what God wanted us to say? Because the spirit instructed us through prophecy. Our spirits also witnessed with the Spirit.

We looked at what we wrote. We compared our words against one another, distilled them. We measured our versions, our opinions. We weighed them against others. We talked about their meaning, literal and spiritual. Does the story refer to itself, or does it have a larger frame of reference? How does it match up with tradition?

"But what if God is doing something new?"

"With everyone writing, there will be a lot to choose from."

"Our writing has to carry the opinions and contradictions."

"Not all witnesses will agree. There has to be room for interpretation."

"What if there is misinterpretation?"

"God marks his word with an act of grace. It can be discerned."

---

1. John 8:6–8.

Prudah

One evening, the potter came to visit my father. I couldn't hear what they said. I sat in the next room watching a little spot of light move up the wall. The potter was asking something. My father was insistent.

I watched the potter leave our door.

I felt the blackness in an empty ship's cargo hold, though I had never been inside a ship, only watched them being unloaded from the shore. I felt pulled away from the one light I wanted.

The next morning, I could not rise from bed, though my sisters tried to pull me up.

Could I give up all things for Christ? Even what I wanted above all others?

No, I was not worthy. He would have to take it from me. I could not give it up willingly. He would have to use fire.

Our mother continued to sit with us, but more often she stayed in her room. It was the fear brought on by our dangerous position. She heard many voices in the market speaking out against the Christians. We could be taken from our homes. We could be fed to lions.

"You'll always find voices trying to invent their own truth," our father said.

"But how do you know your truth?" our mother asked.

"The witness of the Christ, his followers, the Holy Spirit, the prophets, the Scriptures. He is the one sent from God for the remission of our sins."

"And what is my sin?" she asked. "I have been faithful to you. I have raised four daughters."

My father tried to piece together what Stephen said before the Sanhedrin for her.

"Yes, and it got him stoned," she answered.

Our mother stopped coming out from her room. Often she was feverish, and we saw her tremble when we took meals to her.

She died suddenly and unexpectedly one evening as the light from the sea turned pink in the room.

She was buried in a grave lined with stones outside Caesarea. My father led the service.

We began our days of mourning.

We wondered why there had been no warning, no prophecy of her death.

Uprising of Goats

"There is prophecy that is not in another tongue," Clauda said.

"Did not Elizabeth prophesy when Mary entered her house?"[2] Philipa asked.

"Did not Anna prophesy in the temple when Jesus' parents brought him, saying that redemption had come to Israel?"[3] Lucina said. "Did not Zacharias prophesy over his son, John?"[4]

It isn't always in a different language.

I am come to set fire on the earth; and what will I, if it be already kindled? But I have a baptism to be baptized with; and how I am constrained till it be accomplished.

—Luke 12:49–50

Lucina cried out in sleep. We thought she was crying for our mother, but she was dreaming. In the dream, she said she rose from the bed carrying our shells back to the sea.

"How many shells are there on the shore?" she asked.

Women were the lesser. Women were seashells, those bones of the sea.

My father was the lesser among disciples and apostles. Didn't they know what he did?

I thought Christianity was for whoever could bear disappointment. It was for those who were willing to battle. It was for those who could believe what they couldn't see. Who could accept what was not logical. What was beyond belief: that this world was a little pond in which we prepared for the world beyond this one. Christianity was for those who could believe that.

When we worked, I felt the bones that ran like fire through our writing.

It was Rome that ruled Caesarea. "I will support Caesar Augustus, his children and descendants, throughout my life, in word, deed and thought . . .

---

2. Luke 1:42.
3. Luke 2:36–38.
4. Luke 1:67.

Prudah

and whomsoever they regard as enemies I will attack and pursue with arms and the sword, by land and by sea"[5] was an oath that was written there.

It was Herod who built Caesarea. He persecuted believers, as Paul had done. Herod killed James, the brother of John. He imprisoned Peter, but Peter escaped. Then Herod had the guards put to death.

We prayed for the families of the guards, their children, their wives, and their unmarried daughters. We prayed for those whom Herod had tormented.

Then Herod came from Judea to Caesarea. He stood on the rostrum, the royal portico, in his royal robes. The people shouted to him. "He was a god," they said. But he fell dead in front of them all. Herod was killed as he had killed. Dead as he made dead.

Philip, our father, read to us in the evening from Deut 4:24, "The Lord is a consuming fire."

I will kindle a fire in the forest and it shall consume everything around it.

—JER 21:14

We stood on faith, no matter what. We knew some of the apostles were imprisoned. One was on an island. What would happen? We lived moral lives, stayed away from idols, visited with Paul, and waited for Christ, though he had not returned. What was holding him? Did he find something else to do? Had he forgotten us?

Maybe the sea was our brother. Or our husband.

In the marketplace, I could not pass the potter's house.

What would happen when our father died? Who would support us? Should one of us marry in case Jesus didn't return before our death?

Would we be paupers? Paul was in our house again for a meeting with the guards. Felix agreed to let Paul come and go. Would Paul let us breathe? Did he hear our prophecies? Did he think we should prophesy?

We still mourned for our mother. Her turbulence left an emptiness in the house. Sometimes we were silent as we thought of her. Other times we talked about her, remembering how she haggled with the merchants in the marketplace and taught us to bake.

---

5. E. A. Judge, "The Decrees of Caesar," *Reformed Theological Review* 30 (1971) 4.

Uprising of Goats

After the death of our mother and our time of mourning—after the letters and prayers—my father decided we would go to Hierapolis in Asia Minor with the others, because of the need for disciples there.

And so it came to pass. We sold our house in Caesarea and gave away our belongings. How could we leave without looking back? Nevertheless, I felt the wind from the sea that would lift us from Caesarea.

We walked along the pier to the ship through the boxes of cargo and the clutter of all that still had to be loaded. We stepped around crates, bundles, baskets, tethered animals. I wanted to turn back, but we had already given away our bundles.

We carried small parcels for our trip to Asia. It was more than a trip, because a trip implied a return. It was thought we would not see Caesarea, or our mother's grave, ever again.

Paul had been in prison for two years in Caesarea, where he would later be beheaded. We wouldn't see him again either, or at least, not until we reached heaven.

And so, we boarded ship for Asia Minor.

More than once, we turned to look back—to see for one last time what we had seen all our lives, taking for granted that it would always be there. The spilling waves, the rushing wind, and the roar of the sea.

I looked back for the potter as we left, but I did not see him.

We traveled two weeks in the rocking ship, staying close to shore as we traveled. In the night, it seemed to me that even the water was on fire. A fire without light. Jesus could be the ballast that steadied it. My three sisters and I followed our father.

On the crossing, we saw into hell with our prophecies. We had visions in our dreams. The tortured swallowed a meal of fireballs. That was their supper. Not figs or dates or fish or cakes, but fire. Dark beings licked the undersides of their feet with their hot tongues.

It was the noise more than anything. The howlings and screamings. I held my hands to my ears, but the noise still racked my head.

That was why we believed. That was why we followed the doctrine of belief. To avoid hell—a sea of fire the waves continually poured onto shore, drenching our feet. A firestorm. A storm of fire.

"Yes," Philip, our father, said. "We believed to be with Christ."

We saw sickness everywhere on the ship. Young mothers unable to nurse their young ones. The crippled. Jaws swollen with toothache. Earache. Various deformities.

Prudah

I ask you, Lord, that there be joy in our house.

I ask you, Lord, to quell the high voices.

I ask, Lord, for peace like the flood that lifted Noah and his family in his ark, with all the animals floating there.

I ask, Lord, that you bless my sisters.

I ask, Lord, that you not take them from me, else I will have no one.

I ask, Lord, that you provide our meat.

Provide the hope of our calling above.

Keep uplifting us as we are lifted upon the waves.

Steady our minds. Quiet our fears. They rise like ashes from the pile of burning fish bones on the shore.

Bless us, O Lord, with visions of heaven. How your space goes on and on. How we will worship you.

You have given us fire.

You fill our hollow places with your Comforter.

We have not been hungry.

We have not been bereft.

We sat at the funeral of our mother. We praised you, Lord. You have smoothed her bones. You have lifted her into the sky, where you are tetrarch. Where you are above Herod and the awful acts of men.

We have seen men flogged.

We have heard the crowds cry out for the death of the believers.

I have seen a blind man fall over crates scattered near the wharf. He is one we prayed for, and his blindness did not depart.

"*Whoommrobatusedambrieto.*" I heard my sister speak in tongues.

Who knows who we worship? This strange God who sends others in his place. Christ and the Comforter. They are his friends. They are the doers of his will.

If only they had been daughters.

I call out to you, O Lord of Hosts. You know we are feeble. You know we cannot be without you. We would seek you under the sea. We would lift its edge as if a coverlet on our bed. We would find you in the deep. We would ride in a whale. We would drown.

We saw the unexpected storms, the changing shades of water. The waves were battered by the wind. In turn, they battered. They were wakened by the wind.

Lucina said she heard the fish crying as we crossed the water.

I had watched the ships all my life, now I stood upon one, holding to a post. Now we were sailing to Miletus on the long journey to Hierapolis. From Miletus we would travel to Laodicea and on to Hierapolis.

The sea was calm, but Clauda was sick most of the way. For some reason, I could stand the rocking of the ship on the water. It was the thought of nothing under us but the water we could step through. If it tipped, the water would run into the boat and we would sink to the bottom. We would pass the fish, who would look at us strangely.

We prayed for Clauda.

We prayed for all of us as we left the Caesarea we had known all our lives. We had thought we would die there and be buried with our mother. Maybe a husband would be in Hierapolis for us. Maybe one would be ahead. I had the thought too, but we had our work: prophesying. Saying what the Comforter wished us to say.

At night the stars rolled over the sky. The sky, full of lights, was an upside down sea. We saw falling stars and cloudy streams through the dark. Their streaks of fire. Chariots with angels in them coming to earth to help the lame, the weak, and the blind.

"Have you ever seen an angel in a chariot?" Philipa asked, disgusted with our impracticability.

"Who knows what we have seen?"

"How do you know there are not angels riding on this boat in the name of the Crucified One?"

"Should we dress as men when we travel in Asia?"

"We do not look like men. We would be found out."

"The Lord will protect us."

"Could we prophesy if we were not virgins?"

"Yes—married women prophesied."

At night, we heard the ocean speak.

The ship carried animals. At night, we heard them sing. They were weary. They were afraid. They sang because of their fear.

God visits the beasts also. He tamed the lion. He ministered to the fish.

Lucina prayed for the beasts. She baptized them with seawater. She spoke to them and they spoke to her. That is what she said.

Sometimes in the dark of the cargo hold, we called our father, Philip. We wanted to make sure he was there. We were afraid God would call him into heaven like Elijah and we would be left alone.

Prudah

After several days, we saw land and a town by the sea. We stood on deck as the ship made its way into port.

After we landed in Miletus, we spent several more days journeying overland with camels and donkeys. We came to a white-rocked mountain. A cliff rose above us, on top of which sat Hierapolis. We looked up with open mouths.

"The moon has fallen on the earth," Philipa said.

"Goat's milk has spilled," said Clauda.

The mountainside was covered with mineral deposits that flowed from the springs. The hill looked like the white waves that washed into Caesarea.

"We didn't lose the sea after all," Lucina said.

We set up house in Hierapolis.

We joined the Christian women who belonged to a guild of purple dyers. Not the purple from the ink sack of the shellfish, but a purple dye made from a plant and the mineral waters of the springs.

We were strengthened by Scriptures. We felt a calling to do what we were doing. We were grateful for our place. The Christians in the small meeting in Hierapolis looked to us for our prophecies.

We ate salted fish, and in the evenings we looked through the cypress into the valley across the plain to the west, toward the sea.

We had come to Hierapolis.

In the end, I tell you, we were lost among the stars. But we met together in the teetering room that was this earth, and when we prayed, the arms that would hold us forever opened, and we fell into them.

Lucina

BLESSED IS THE WILDNESS of the sea. The beating waves. The shore that receives the pounding. Blessed is the God who stirs the water. Who rules the stormy waves. Blessed are the boats that float upon the mind that is the water. Blessed is the night. Blessed are the fish that surface in the night. Wild beasts come to the sea, but they cannot drink. Only the fish swallow salt water. Blessed is the God who made them love the salt so much they cannot survive outside it. How they fight before they die to get back to it. By eating fish, we take the salt water into ourselves and hunger for the deep. We dream at night as the fish move within us. We feel them swim. In our dreams we become the fish. We swim in the dark under-part of the mind until the sun blinds our sight with its brightness. It covers the sea, and the fish that come up in nets and squirm until their eyes are small inkwells.

It was we four daughters of Philip who wrote what the apostles and travelers said as they passed through our house in Caesarea. It was we daughters who wrote our father's travels.

I also wrote what I wanted to write. About the fish and the beasts. The animals in the marketplace are not the beasts I mean. The wild beasts that call from the wilderness—they are the prophecies I give.

I was the fourth of my father's four daughters: Philipa, Clauda, Prudah, and me, Lucina. My father, Philip, was an evangelist, a fish for Jesus dead on the cross, his eye open to the heavens. My father, Philip, was one of the seven chosen to serve in the upper room in Jerusalem after the death of Christ, the apostles being too busy.

Jesus came with peace. He came with turmoil. How was it both?

I thought the church was an awful place built on blood and death and nails hammered into hands and feet. There was such suffering in it. I saw

Lucina

the other girls in Caesarea marrying, having children. No one came for me. Or any of my sisters. We were virgins and would be. Who would come near our family? Who would believe as we did? Philip, my father, wouldn't let any men look at us unless Christ was their savior and they were filled with the Holy Spirit. They had to perform miracles before they could smile at me. My father scared the young men with the gospel. How could they come into our house? How could I talk to them? I didn't want to prophesy, yet I heard the words in my mouth. Maybe I was just following Philipa, as usual. It seemed to me that Clauda and Lucina followed her too.

Philipa watched the birds when she didn't know what to do. Clauda plodded like a camel. Prudah scoured the Scriptures for the drowned voices of women she could set on fire. I, Lucina, was a wild beast in the wilderness of the sea.

We were dead fish on the shore that no one wanted. Prophecy was our husband.

Sometimes I saw our savior's two round eyes on the sides of his head, his gills sucking air.

In Caesarea, there was a prostitute in the marketplace. I watched her skirts. I imagined her face under her veil. What would it be like? My father read from Isaiah: "A thirsty man dreams and drinks in his dream, but when he wakes, he still is thirsty" (Isa 29:8). I felt heat rising to my face. Maybe he knew what I was thinking.

I had something else to think about. I felt it, yes. I didn't know what it was, but I knew it was coming. It was a lifting I felt. A new language was in our mouths. We spoke in another language without knowing what we spoke. What did I say? There was prophecy in tongues, and then the interpretation of it. How could I speak something I didn't know? How could I interpret something I didn't understand? But that was the lesson. It was not from us, but the Holy Spirit, the Comforter, who had come.

The Holy Ghost came to us when the Apostle Peter came to Caesarea. That warty centurion, Cornelius, had a vision: "Send for Peter, bring him here." It was hard for Peter to hear that Gentiles had a part in God's kingdom. It was hard for Peter to see that even women had a part. As Peter spoke, the Holy Spirit fell on all of us, though we were women, and we spoke with other tongues and magnified God.

The fish in the sea say hello. The whale sends its greeting. It is weightless in the sea.

The lovely foam on the shore is from the lace-maker sea.

Uprising of Goats

The young men knew who we were: Philip's daughters, virgins who spoke a strange language. Who belonged to that strange religion. That place not on earth. Who would want to be with us?

It was a parting from my dreams.

Then the Apostle Paul and his company came to Caesarea. Squatty. Focused. Self-possessed. His eye on the cross. It would make more work for us.

We made his papyrus, filled his ink well. Then he dictated his letters to us. Or we made copies of them for him. We washed his garments and those of his company; we went to the market for them. Listened to them talk. We, the invisible ones here in the corner of our own house. We, the beasts of burden. We, the servants. We, the goats in the marketplace. They just wanted what we had. We were suppliers for their mission, for which they would take the credit. The pressure to give, to share. I was tired of it. Sapphira was my wish. She sold her land, kept the money, and wouldn't give it to them (Acts 5:1–11).

The Apostle Paul came back to our house in Caesarea. Paul, who had tried to drown the church when he was still called Saul. In the beginning, the disciples had scattered because of Paul's persecution of Christians. Now Paul, the persecutor, was persecuted. He had been beaten. He had been let down over a wall in a basket to make his escape. He had been stoned. He had feared for his life. Now he knew how it felt. Now Paul was at our house. Paul, who had torn up the world after Christ. We knew we were surrounded by those who didn't care, or those who wanted us dead. By those who spoke behind our backs when we walked in the marketplace. Who spit. We told ourselves stories to ignore them. Sometimes I spit back.

When Jesus was a boy, he played on the roof of a house of a friend, but the boy fell and his parents found him dead on the street. The other boys ran, but Jesus stayed. The parents screamed that Jesus had pushed him off the roof. Jesus went down to the street and looked at the boy.

"Did I push you?" he asked.

"No," the boy answered as he stood up, to the amazement of his parents. Yes, we told stories. We, who were to be silent in church. Who were observers of their acts. Who were below the consideration of Paul and his company, though we were filled with the Holy Spirit and spoke in other tongues.

I wanted to wish a Scripture on them: "But the word of the Lord was unto them precept upon precept, line upon line—here a little, and there a

Lucina

little; that they might go and fall backward, and be broken, and snared, and taken" (Isa 28:10). The word spares us. It condemns us. It can work both ways.

I wanted to write about my father, Philip. About what he had done and continued to do. He was one of the first disciples to go to the outposts. He preached salvation. He founded churches. But Peter stepped in and questioned him. Peter wanted to edify my father. He wanted everyone to be filled with the Holy Spirit. I heard Peter argue with my father. I heard him correct my father in my father's own house. But I saw my father's ministry to the outcasts. I saw my father's lowly place. Does Paul or Peter know how many people responded to my father? Philip, the overlooked. Philip, the humble servant. Philip, the minister to the outcast, the discarded, the poor, the ignorant, the lepers, the lame, the blind, the weak, the women.

Jesus was publicly executed with common criminals. He was judged and condemned by Rome. Dismissed by scholars. My father has suffered like Christ.

I roared like a beast. I groaned. I hissed. I made a high-pitched cry.

My father prayed for my outbreaks. I was my mother's daughter. Terrible with wildness. I felt her trailing us when we left Caesarea for Hierapolis. Some nights I felt her above the ship. I knew she traveled the road beside us, though she was in another world.

I must not shout! I must be quiet so he can't find me—this Jesus who tamed the fire. All the rowdiness in this quiet house. All this writing. The stylus scratching the papyrus. Does the papyrus suffer like us?

The stories roll by: His father was a carpenter making ploughs and yokes, but a man asked him to make a ladder. He cut one side shorter than the other by mistake and did not know what to do. He laid the two pieces side by side. He grasped the shorter side and stretched it to match the longer.

James, Jesus' brother, was gathering wood when a snake bit him, but Jesus breathed on the snake with its mouth still clamped on James' hand. The snake burst, and James was healed.

Noah the waterman took wild animals on his boat, and tied the whales behind, and had underwater cages to drag the fish with him to Ararat. I prophesied and looked to see who was looking and what they would say.

God brought light to the waters. Before there was a sun, he brought light, and the division between light and its darkness. What was not night was day, and he called them day and night. He made dryness for the land and wetness for the sea. He held them together on his hand, and gave them certain places—*you stay here, and you there, and cannot mix*—though the waves washed over the evening that seemed light and dark becoming one. He went on dividing the lesser light to rule the night, and the greater light to rule the day. I sat as the lesser sister in our meeting alongside the lesser Philip, my father, as the apostles in Caesarea set bounds.

Clauda was sick when she was a child. Philipa said they held her as if she were the baby. They rocked her while I cried in my infant's bed. I must have heard her screams above mine. But it passed, and she is docile. She left the howling with me. The wild beasts come in the night. Not all of them at once, but one of them or two: a leopard and its mate. Or beasts I don't know. Many have come and gone. What is done to the little ones stay with them. The war between the earth and the sea. The sea was going to cover the earth, but God said the sea had to stay a certain place. It can come so far and no farther. The sea can't cover us because God said it couldn't, and it has to listen to God. It does.

Prudah found a stone with an indention for an inkwell. We learned to make papyrus on which we copied the words of others. We learned to write our own words. I felt I had to document everything we said, or else no one would listen. Scriptures were like little pools within the rocks of our writing.

Paul, the tentmaker, wasn't making many tents with us.

In the evening we read our writings of the day aloud. Philipa hogged the oil lamp. Our words were like fish swimming in the sea. Our words were fish swimming. Sometimes we flopped on the shore of our faith like fish.

God loved the beasts of the wilderness. Was not the old tabernacle covered with skins? Badger skins? Yes, God brought into his kingdom the wild beasts. Prophecy is when the wild beasts call.

I wanted to write how it is in these confusing days. I wanted to write of the insertions I felt from another place. We thought Jesus would call his kingdom to the earth, but he left us abandoned. He left us mocked by the people in the marketplace, scorned by our neighbors. It was only in our meeting in Caesarea that we found community when the Spirit fell on us. It was in Hierapolis too—we know the *salt-giver* Christ came to us there.

He washed us in his blood—was this like the women washing their clothes?

Jesus the lamb. What makes the others not know Christ? What makes the magistrates who pass in splendor in the streets with their train of guards remain behind their curtained litters? Felix. Festus. King Agrippa. What made Naaman, the leper, the Ethiopian eunuch, and the Samaritan believe?

I listened to the Scriptures my father read in our meetings. I took notes.

He gathered the waters.

He gave the sea its decree.

He compassed the waters with a boundary.

I have placed the sand for the bound for the sea that it cannot pass.

The sea saw it and fled.

From Caesarea, we called out to the sea. Philipa had the loudest voice.

The Lord is mightier than the noise of the sea.

He rules the raging of the sea. When the waves thereof arise, he stills them.

We called out to the sea—he stills the waves of the sea.

In Hierapolis, I had a heaviness I couldn't lift. I missed the sea. My father and sisters prayed for me. I tried to be happy as we played with the children, but I could not. I wanted to lie on my bed and not get up. I wanted the sea to wash over me, but it was far from us. Sometimes I looked at my collection of shells. Maybe the sea was calling them back. Maybe I could go with them.

Darkness was a shape in which other things happened.

I puzzled over questions. The demons begged Jesus not to be sent out of the country, but rather into a herd of swine who jumped over the cliff and drowned in the sea. Why did they not want to be sent out of the country? Why did they prefer to drown in the sea? What would I do without the water? In Caesarea, we had read letters from Hierapolis, where my father wanted to go. Inland. Inland—away from the sea—I had heard it all my life. I wanted to drown in the sea. No, I wouldn't go. There were too many obstacles in the way. But here I am in Hierapolis.

I felt the fish that ran through our writing.

Our new life was a sea, something you could stand beside, something that could swallow you, that had creatures in it you could never dream of. And prophecy—I was afraid of it.

Prophecy was a net of creatures from underwater.

A Chapter in Which There Is an Afterword to the Daughters of Philip

You cannot not put yourself in.

—A. S. Byatt, "Ghosts and Documents"

Philip was one of the first disciples to leave Jerusalem for the purpose of evangelism. He was a *pioneering missionary*."[1]

—F. Scott Spencer, *The Portrait of Philip in Acts: A Study of Roles and Relations*

Maybe Philip wanted to travel away from those first difficult days after the crucifixion with the message: *All was not lost. Jesus was alive!* Maybe Philip was a wanderer, a nomad. Maybe he was one to act on his own and not wait for the group. In my research, I found an early letter from Peter reproaching Philip for his absence from them.[2]

It seems that Philip was in Jerusalem during the time of Pentecost. Afterwards, he set out again. He went to Samaria. From Samaria, he was

---

1. F. Scott Spencer, *The Portrait of Philip in Acts: A Study of Roles and Relations*, Journal for the Study of the New Testament Supplement Series 67 (Sheffield, UK: Sheffield Academic, 1992) 272.

2. Ibid., 242.

A Chapter in Which There Is an Afterword to the Daughters of Philip

directed by an angel to go to the road from Jerusalem to Gaza, where he met the Ethiopian eunuch. Next he was in Azotus, then in Caesarea by the end of Acts 8.

Who was Philip? He had a Greek name, but he was probably a Jew who spoke Greek. What was his trade? Was he from Jerusalem? Was he from someplace else? The more I read, the more I thought Philip was likely from Jerusalem. He was probably alone in Jerusalem at the time of the crucifixion. Maybe he met his wife in Caesarea. She was another mystery. Not only did she not have a name, she was not even mentioned. Was it an unhappy marriage? Was divorce not an option for her? Did she not go along with his faith? Christians were not part of the larger society. They were often outcasts. They feared imprisonment and beatings. They feared for their lives. Christianity itself was full of rifts and disagreements.

What was this new religion? The confusion everyone felt after the crucifixion had been resolved in some ways, because Jesus was seen alive, but the basic tenets had not yet been put into place. Could Gentiles be part of the kingdom? Could Samaritans, old enemies of the Jews, be accepted by God? No. Yes. Those were the answers.

It seems that Philip spent many years in Caesarea, where he had:

> ... a flourishing family of four daughters, all of them a credit to their father, for they were prophetesses, every one. Some years later Philip and his daughters, with other Palestinian Christians, immigrated to the province of Asia and spent their remaining days there. The daughters—or some of them at least—lived to a great age, and were highly esteemed as informants on persons and events belonging to the early years of Judean Christianity ... This information we owe to Papias, bishop of Asian Hierapolis, quoted by Eusebius.[3]

In my research, I found there was confusion between Philip the apostle and Philip the evangelist, who is first mentioned in Acts 6:5–6 as one of the seven chosen to do work the apostles were too busy to do. This was an unprecedented time. Thousands were being converted. People were selling all they had and sharing with the poor.

Did the other Philip, the apostle, have daughters too?

3. F. F. Bruce, *The Book of the Acts*, New International Commentary on the New Testament (Grand Rapids: Eerdmans, 1966) 423–24, n. 11.

Uprising of Goats

> In Asia, great luminaries have fallen asleep, such as shall rise again on the day of the Lord's appearing, when He comes in glory from heaven to seek out all his saints; to wit, Philip, one of the twelve apostles, who has fallen asleep in Hierapolis, [as have] also his two daughters who grew old in virginity, and his other daughter who lived in the Holy Spirit and rests at Ephesus . . .[4]

> Tradition holds that Philip the evangelist and his daughters did not remain in Caesarea. Of the numerous strands, one found in Eusebius is that the four women were also prophetesses in Hierapolis in Asia and that their graves as well as their father's were pointed out there toward the end of the second century. Although many recognize the confusion in Eusebius (or his sources) between Philip the apostle and Philip the evangelist, F. F. Bruce's considered opinion judges that this particular Eusebian tradition does apply to the evangelist. Another strand of Christian lore, found in the *Menologion of Basil II*, holds that Philip and his daughters moved to Tralles where Philip became bishop.[5]

Several afternoons, I sat in the library in confusion as to which Philip was in Asia Minor. Or could it have been both? It didn't seem likely.

How far could I go in imagining the *acts* of the four daughters?

> According to Eusebius and Philip of Side, Papias told on the authority of Philip's daughters how this man [Joseph called Barsabbas, one of the two nominated, but not elected, to replace Judas as the twelfth disciple] when challenged by unbelievers, drank serpent's poison in the Lord's name with no harmful consequences.[6]

Does that mean *the four* were in the upper room? Where else would they have met Barsabbas? It seems unlikely that they were in Jerusalem during Pentecost. Maybe they heard it from their father or someone who visited them in Caesarea.

---

4. Eusebius, *Hist. eccl.* 5.24.2–7, translated by H. J. Lawlor and J. E. L. Oulton, *Eusebius, Bishop of Caesarea: The Ecclesiastical History and the Martyrs of Palestine* (London: SPCK, 1927) 1:169.

5. Florence M. Gillman, *Women Who Knew Paul* (Collegeville, MN: Liturgical Press, 1992) 80. See also F. F. Bruce, *The Epistles to the Colossians, to Philemon, and to the Ephesians*, New International Commentary on the New Testament (Grand Rapids: Eerdmans, 1984).

6. F. F. Bruce, *The Acts of the Apostles: The Greek Text with Introduction and Commentary* (Grand Rapids: Eerdmans, 1951) 79.

A Chapter in Which There Is an Afterword to the Daughters of Philip

In my research and reading, there were other accounts of Philip, again with the possibility of the two Philips having been confused. One of my readings, the *Acts of Philip*, was an apocryphal text of events. Possibly, if the events were included in the New Testament, they would subvert focus on the straightforward message of the gospels: "I am come that you might have life" (John 10:10). In the first Act of Philip, he resurrected a woman's son by the power of his God, Jesus Christ. The son told of tortures he saw in the underworld: a woman resembling a dragon, an angel with a sword of fire and frying pan. In the third Act of Philip, he heard an eagle speaking. During his passage to Azotus, locusts attacked his ship. Philip called out to his merciful Lord, Jesus Christ. A light shone brighter than the sun and illuminated the sea: "Sea monsters, fish, and beasts form a circle and made obeisance to the light, howling hymns in their language. The sea is changed by the majesty of the light, the air becomes still, and the locusts die in the sea."[7] Magical, mythical leopards, dragons, and snakes speak praises and other illuminations in the further Acts of Philip.

What stayed with me were comments such as:

> According to a later tradition, Philip's daughters transmitted accurate knowledge of the early days—perhaps some of the material in the Acts of the Apostles—and modern scholars even suspect that the accounts of Jesus' life in the Gospels took shape at Caesarea. Could some of the actual words have been written by the four? Could Philip's daughters have kept journals of the events of their father's evangelism? Could Philip have shared with Luke the information his daughters logged as Luke was writing his own gospel as well as the book of Acts? Luke seems to indicate that his writings came from several sources. There is testimony of this in the opening verses of Luke: "Forasmuch as many have taken in hand to set forth in order a declaration of those things which are most surely believed among us. Even as they delivered them unto us" (Luke 1:1-2).[8]

Also, there's the possibility that Philip played an important part in the later narrative of Acts. Luke may have been indebted to him for some of the material of Acts.[9]

---

7. Kenneth G. Holum et al., eds., *King Herod's Dream: Caesarea on the Sea* (New York: Norton, 1988) 224, n. 14.

8. Ibid., 158.

9. F. F. Bruce, *The Book of the Acts*, New International Commentary on the New Testament (Grand Rapids: Eerdmans, 1966) 129, n. 6.

Uprising of Goats

The summer after Baylor, I went to Caesarea and Turkey on a travel grant. I flew into the body of heaven. I felt summoned to another land to write about the history there. These voices. These missing historical texts.

I heard the call to substantiate the unsubstantiated—to fabricate historical voices. A cloak for the invisible. Goat hair for the bolsters. Honey from the carcass of a lion. The barely mentioned. They rise up. They speak.

I heard their little goat-cries in my half-sleep. A revisionary of something not known. Not recorded—sometimes not even named—not said—except that they were there—voiceless as the ocean below the plane . . .

I continued to think about the book—about how the different voices would fit together. I used the travel grant to cover the cost of the plane ticket and hotel in Hierapolis and Caesarea in a time of *intifada* after the atrocities of the American invasion of Iraq. After the abuse of Iraqi prisoners at Abu Ghraib during the Iraqi war. The tortures at Guantanamo. In Turkey, I saw an American flag hanging upside down. In Israel, my purse was scanned at restaurant doors.

What was it like for the daughters of Philip to move from the littoral setting to inland mountains? In Hierapolis I climbed a steep hill to the ruins of the *Martyrium Philip*, where I sat on the stone seats and faced the lectern.

I understood the ways of storytelling for these four daughters of Philip—how many voices could come together to tell a story. Or stories. The four daughters went with their father, Philip, to Hierapolis in Asia, which was now in western Turkey. They did not go. Their mother died. Their mother lived and went with them.

In travel, I had encountered the daughters as if, two thousand years ago, I were entering their house in Caesarea as they pondered the perplexing events of the death of Christ, his resurrection, and the rowdy aftermath that took place as those of faith tried to sort through the possibilities and face their fears of persecution and death. They expected Christ would return for them at any time. Yet he delayed. What had they not understood?

I see these writings of these four sisters as fragments of the first literature of the new world that began with the death and resurrection of Jesus Christ. As linguistic anthropologist Dell Hymes observes, "the point of having stories was for those who encounter them to make them their own,"[10] reminding us of the words of the Dutch theologian Edward Schillebeeckx: "telling stories properly also involved being caught up in them . . . in the end what we are concerned with is the fusing of two stories, the story of the gospel tradition of faith and the story of our own personal and communal life."[11]

As Hymes goes on to explain:

> Denis Demert, a Tlingit educator, once remarked that the Tlingit know there were different local versions of certain historical events, but that was not a problem until one version was written down and as a result was taken as the one true one. Yet forces [of] diversity have been present in both Native and Judeo-Christian communities. It is well known that the several canons, Jewish and Christian, have existed within a large field of other works.[12]

Many stories of the flood flood the cultures of the earth.

Among the possibilities, among all of what could have happened, I imagined. I traveled to the place. I listened. I posited my text in the context of air and called it solid ground.

How could I keep writing first-person stories about women who had lived? I had to be more separated from the pedestrian. Could I insert my words into the daughters' heads? Or would theirs come into mine? Could I use a postmodern entry into an old story? Could I talk about writing a fiction based on unknown nonfiction, which was, therefore, fiction? How far could I go on imagining the *acts* of each one of the four daughters?

I lived a bifurcated life, keeping the heads of biblical women in my head. As a pregnant woman has two heads.

He was there in the wilderness forty days with the wild beasts. He was in the sea.

Often when I finished a section, I felt I had been underwater for a long time. I felt out of breath. I felt I was gasping for air.

---

10. Dell Hymes, *Now I Know Only So Far: Essays in Ethnopoetics* (Lincoln: University of Nebraska Press, 2003) 6.

11. John Bowden, *Edward Schillebeeckx: Portrait of a Theologian* (London: SCM, 1983) 134–35.

12. Dell Hymes, *Now I Know Only So Far: Essays in Ethnopoetics* (Lincoln: University of Nebraska Press, 2003) 7.

Uprising of Goats

When I returned first from Waco, and then later Turkey, my colleagues were distant. So this was the price. Suspicion of my interests and independence. The distancing of my work from the others. *Ostracization*—I made up words. I felt the same way Philip probably felt when he read the reproaches in the letter from Peter. Maybe they had quarrels over something unrelated to the problem.

That was my fear—in the end, I would be the only one in my world. In the midst of my despondency, Walker called and said that he planned to remarry. I had not seen him in church for a while, but didn't realize he was attending church with someone else. It was another stab of loss. Maybe divorce was not necessary, but at the time, I felt it was. I knew my former mother-in-law would die. I would be next. Both my parents were gone. My daughters would be busy with their own families, or their work, or both. There still would be students I heard from now and then. We would have lunch. I would go back to my house alone.

It was the problem of being dipped in the world. To know that I was nothing on the grand scale. The college, the country even, the leader of the world, took a backseat in rural Turkey. They wanted economic stability. Money. Income. A house in which to live. Something to eat. Security for the children. The ceasing of war. Of cruelty. Of fear. What did my book mean to that? I was from a privileged country. I could make up voices. I could think of something other than survival.

What was this faith, this underpinning of Christianity in a Christian land? I saw the churches everywhere. I saw faith that my college was trying to squash, or ignore, or not allow, or at least, treat as something to be looked at with suspicion. There was that word again. I was suspicious of these voices. Were they parts of me? Maybe I worried that I was losing my mind. Submerging into these women. Would I go mad with voices? Would I be kept in an institution different from the college where I taught? That's where mad women were kept. Would my department put me at the end of the hall in a room they hoped no one passed? Would I be removed? I had tenure. I had tenure, I reminded myself again, but it was still possible. It had happened. In those stories of faculty gone bizarre and gradually shuffled away.

I felt the floggings. The persecutions. The fear of loss. I felt the sewing in my hands. My fingers worked with threads.

I had the discomfort of research in another institution. The heat. The squalid poverty of being by oneself. The loss of habit. Of comfort. Of the feeling of arrival. Why was I doing this? Was I the chosen? Would I be

A Chapter in Which There Is an Afterword to the Daughters of Philip

unruly with holiness? Would I lie in the street with papers to grade lined up through eternity? What was the everlasting into which I would step? Would I ever meet these lovely voices that convened in my head?

Teaching began again the fall, as though I had never had a sabbatical, nor been across the sea. Yet I had written a body of work, a manuscript held together with a strong binder clip.

I sat in my office one afternoon with my hands on my desk, waiting for another voice I felt would appear. Only then I could continue writing, but no one came that afternoon. I picked up the book we would discuss in my next class and made a few notes until I found myself daydreaming. If I closed my office door, maybe students wouldn't realize I had returned from sabbatical.

This is what would happen. I would publish the manuscript of the voices of biblical women. Justine Crowd would assign it in her class and the students would read it and be converted. Wake up! It would not happen that way. I pushed myself out of the daydream. Justine would consider the voices of biblical women mythological, and the students would agree. There would be an awkward silence because there was nothing else to discuss.

In the past, I had assigned books I hadn't read. It wasn't a good idea. I read reviews, of course. I paged through copies at the bookstore. But often, the book didn't turn out like I hoped, and I hurried to get through it. I had to keep up with my reading. Therefore, I assigned the books I hadn't read. Sometimes the students got something out of it. Reading their papers, I saw a perspective I hadn't seen. Other books, which I thought were seminal, the students didn't like.

Often, I got involved with their lives. Several students would hold a discussion in my office, or one student would continue something they didn't have a chance to finish in class. There always was a sense of expectancy: Who would walk into my office next? What would the issue be?

One day in my office, after the last advisee left, I opened my file cabinet and looked through old manuscripts, which I returned to their folders. One of them, *Biblical Texts, Christian Narratives*, I left on my desk for a day or two before I returned it to the file cabinet. They were a collection of my lectures from which I thought might make a book. But I didn't want the current manuscript of women's voices to be over yet. I couldn't fabricate a voice. I had to wait for it to appear.

Uprising of Goats

I thought about the relationship of text to place. I thought about the texture of remembered landscape—how it was skewed with subjective perception, or the residue of it was. What was I getting at? The textures of a land never seen: the terrain of the Holy Land of desert and sky and sea. How much one was like another. It was as if it were transposed through writing. I continued to talk about an unreliable memory, a landscape hardly seen but for a brief trip, and how I made a brief and transposed fabric of it.

I hardly counted the short trip to Caesarea and Hierapolis as a trip to the Holy Land. I had never had either the opportunity or the money. I had too many other things to do, and no one else was interested. I had never wanted to go enough to go on my own until I wrote about Philip's daughters. Had I been afraid I'd be blown up by a bomb? I could risk myself for research. The threat of a bomb hadn't been a factor when I was in college. Why had I wanted to hold it all at a distance as an observer, not a partaker? Had my own faith grown distant—yet flamed from time to time like the autumn maples?

I prepared my lectures. I held class. I cleaned the house. I picked up the dry cleaning. I raked leaves. I took the car for an oil change. I paid the bills. I fed the goats. What little noises they made—their banterings, bellowings, natterings, were always there.

It was Justine Crowd dominating the meeting. There were her thoughts on this and her thoughts on that. She was always searching for something new to say, or a new way to say some existing text. To interpret. To download. To reinterpret. The ones with mannerisms and gimmicks showed confidence. They camped out in meetings. They stood talking in the hall.

When a student was killed in a car accident, it was me, not Justine Crowd, who read Scripture at his memorial service, though I had been gone a semester. I sat beside his grieving parents in the college chapel with a feeling of self-satisfaction.

In exposing the voices of these women, I was exposed. My self-satisfaction was a leprosy to me.

MIRIAM

Seven Days in Leprosy Camp
A Chapter Stuck in the Desert

And his sister followed to see what would be done with him.
—Exod 2:4

And Miriam the prophetess led the women in dance.
—Exod 15:20

And Miriam and Aaron spoke against Moses.
—Num 12:1

And Miriam became leprous.
—Num 12:10

And Miriam was shut out of camp.
—Num 12:15

And Miriam died there in Kadesh and was buried.
—Num 20:1

Uprising of Goats

> Remember what the Lord your God did to Miriam after they were come from Egypt.
>
> —Deut 24:9

I HAD NEVER GONE so far into the other world. I needed another language to speak. I needed the spirits to come out of the words and stand by themselves.

Leprosy covered my arms and hands. Under my robe, it covered my body. It looked like the manna we found on the ground. Just because I asked, "Does the Lord speak only by Moses?" Just because I spoke against Moses' wife, who was a Cushite. An Ethiopian. A woman from the desert. At one time, Moses sent her back. But she returned with Jethro, her father—and the two sons like her.

After I criticized—after I questioned—the Lord called Moses, Aaron, and myself to the tabernacle of the congregation. He descended in the pillar of his cloud. He said he would speak to Moses mouth-to-mouth. Not in dreams or visions or similitude, as he did with others. Why were Aaron and I not afraid to speak against Moses? When the cloud departed, I cried out. I was white as snow with leprosy. Aaron and Moses gasped.

Moses pleaded for my healing. But the Lord God said, *If her father had spit in her face, should she not be ashamed seven days?* (Num 12:14).

I looked at horror at my hands and arms—I felt the risings on my face. I was stricken. I wanted the earth to swallow me up. I wanted to sink into it and disappear. I held my veil over my face. My legs trembled and folded to the ground. No one could help me up because of the leprosy. I crawled before I could stand. When I could walk, the crowd parted as I started through them. Just like the sea. I heard a few women cry when I passed. Some let out noises of amazement or shock. The rest were silent.

The Lord God kept me outside the camp for seven days. The Hebrews couldn't move. The Lord God said they had to wait. They couldn't continue the journey from Egypt to Canaan. What would they do, they who were used to moving? What were they saying? "Poor Miriam. She deserves what she got"?

Do they remember how I told them to gather water before the river turned to blood in Egypt? Do they remember my dancing after we crossed

Seven Days in Leprosy Camp

through the Red Sea? I was the first woman to walk between the parted waters. It was holy and terrifying. Do they remember that?

Aaron spoke against our brother's wife. He asked with me, "Is Moses the only one who can speak?" Why wasn't he stricken with leprosy? Why wasn't he put outside the Hebrew's camp? Look at them encamped so orderly around the tabernacle. Listen to their whispers.

Seven days I sat in a tent outside the camp. The Lord God made the world in seven days. The Hebrews would have to wait that long for me. I was angry because they had to wait. I was a leader. Now I sat wrapped in my shame. Was it fair?

There was no pain with leprosy. I was surprised.

Moses was favored. He was raised in Pharaoh's house. But we were slaves. We were oppressed. We worked. We grew in number. Pharaoh told the midwives to kill the Hebrew's sons when they were born. But the midwives did not kill them. When Moses was born, though Moses was not the name she called him, my mother wove a small ark of bulrushes. I watched her fingers. She was more determined than frantic or worried. We daubed the little ark with pitch and slime. She laid the baby in the ark. It sailed from the flags by the river's edge like a rat's nest. I followed, as she told me, to watch where he went (Exod 2:4). I walked near the reeds as though on an errand. I saw a woman come to the river with her servants. It was Pharaoh's daughter. She lifted the ark from the water, and the women saw he was a Hebrew. They admired him. When he cried, I asked if she wanted me to find a nurse among the Hebrew women. Pharaoh's daughter said yes. I went to get my mother.

I thought Moses wrote too much. Day after day. Frowning. Writing. Writing. The book of the law. The book of our groanings. The book of our goings. The women continued to scrape goatskins for parchments, stretching them, tanning them. The Lord spoke to Moses about this. The Lord spoke to Moses about that. The tabernacle was set up such a way, and the laws, all the laws, were given. Moses kept writing: the furniture for the tabernacle. The goat and badger skins for the covering. The priests' robes. Was there no one else to write?

Uprising of Goats

It started in Egypt—with the Egyptian guard Moses killed because he was beating a Hebrew slave. Until then, we had been safe. We had been careful. At night, we listened to stories from my father, Amran, and the elders. Behind the oil lamp, the darkness waved around us like river flags. Sometimes as I felt I was drowning as I fell asleep.

The men talked of Abraham, Isaac, Jacob, and Joseph. Our history passed like a dream. But after the murder, it wasn't the same. Something happened. We were Hebrews in Goshen. Our younger brother, Moses, was a murderer now. My older brother Aaron and I waited to see what would happen. We talked to him on the outskirts and in the bushes.

No, we had not been safe. We feared for our lives. We were beaten, overworked. I gathered stubble in the fields for mortar and brick. The Hebrews groaned. The land itself moaned with us. We were in misery. We prayed to the Lord God, to the God of Abraham, Isaac, and Jacob. We asked for mercy. We asked for deliverance from our slavery. The Hebrews had been in Egypt 430 years—since Joseph was sold into slavery and became Pharaoh's headman. He provided for Jacob, his father, and his brothers, when they moved from Canaan to Egypt during a famine.

Now we provided for the Egyptians.

We cried to God year after year. We were something other than this. I played the timbrel and sang in our quarters. My brothers were Aaron and Moses. Our parents were Amran and Jochebed. We were Levites—priests—though we were slaves in Egypt.

The name of prophetess came to me because I heard the moaning in the field. It was as if the land cried because of our labor. Did not the Lord God say that he heard Abel's blood cry out from the ground? I knew who was suffering. I would sing for them. One night I sang that our bondage was over. I didn't know what I sang, or why. It looked like we always would be slaves. But our release was a certainty I had. Aaron agreed. I thought of my brother, Moses, taken from the water in his little bulrush ark. Pharaoh's daughter named him Moses after Ramos and Tutmose. But the name sounded like the Hebrew word for "drawn out of the water."

At one time, we wondered what our brother was doing in Pharaoh's house. We thought of the food he ate. The clothes he wore. We thought of his privilege. Did he think of us?

Seven Days in Leprosy Camp

Did anyone think of me, shut away in this tent outside the camp? Miriam, a prophetess, sister of Moses, our leader, and of Aaron, our priest. Daughter of the house of Levi.

Did anyone know how our history was a leprosy camp?

The leprosy tent became a remembering tent—a tent where memory stumbled over its past without order. Events from long ago spilled over beside the memories of the recent past. I remembered crossing through the sea. The sting of leper camp. The embarrassment. I remembered the day that Aaron told me the Lord God wanted him to go into the wilderness to meet with Moses. Something was up. I waited in the slave quarters in Goshen.

When Aaron returned, Moses was with him. Moses had seen a burning bush. God called to him out of the fire. He had seen the misery of his people. He would deliver us out of the hands of the Egyptians. We were giddy with delight. Moses was supposed to go to Pharaoh and tell him to let the Hebrews go. Moses balked and asked, "Whom shall I say has sent me?" God answered, *I am that I am*. He told Moses to take up his shepherd's staff, and it turned it into a serpent. Then Moses put his hand into his tunic, and his hand turned leprous as snow. He put it in his tunic again, and it was healed. Moses and Aaron went to Pharaoh, and Aaron cast down his rod and it became a serpent. And Pharaoh's magicians cast down their rods and they became serpents, but Aaron's rod swallowed up their rods.

I put my hand in my robe in the tent outside the camp. I pulled it back out. It was still leprous.

In Egypt, when the water became blood for seven days, I told the Hebrew women to gather water in the water jugs before it happened. I hardly knew what my prophecy meant at the time—but we gathered water. When the river turned to blood, we had water to drink. We did not have to dig by the river for water like the Egyptians, who found none.

Then there were the days of frogs. Pharaoh's magicians, in trying to compete with Aaron and Moses, caused more frogs to cover the land. They came into houses and beds, into kneading troughs and ovens. The frogs died in stinking heaps.

There were lice and flies—swarms of them—but not in Goshen, where we lived.

There were plagues on the cattle, but not in Goshen.

Then there were the boils, but not on us.

Hail and fire came next, beating cattle and servants to death in the fields of the Egyptians.

Then there were the locusts up to their ears.

Then darkness for three days. I told the women to prepare olive oil. I told them darkness was coming. I told them—I told them—and we Hebrews had light in our lamps.

Then Moses said the first-born in Egypt would die. *Take a lamb, sacrifice it, mark the doorpost of your house with its blood. Eat its meat with unleavened bread and bitter herbs, your shoes on your feet, your staff in your hand, ready to go.*

Even the first-born of the cattle died that night.

Often, I uncovered my arms and studied the crusts of leprosy. Often, I heard the little cries of the leprosy sores. What else did I have to do but listen? What did I have to do but remember?

The Lord went before us by day in a pillar of a cloud, and by night, in a pillar of fire. We left Egypt as a mixed multitude. Mostly Hebrews, but some Egyptians came with us. We camped that first night out of Egypt between Migdol and the sea. Pharaoh would know we were trapped. He sent his army after us. The Hebrews were crazed with fear. Have you brought us to the wilderness to die? They cried. Think of the betrayal and abandonment. The anger at being trapped. What are we going to do?

Moses answered, "The Lord will fight for us—"

I tried to repeat his words, but my voice broke with fear.

The angel of God, who went before the camp of Israel, went behind us then, and stood between us and the Egyptians. Moses stretched out his hand over the sea and caused the sea to part by a strong wind all night. The sea became dry land and we crossed at morning between the walls of water on the ground that had been sea.

I was at the head of the line. The water stood up like walls.

Aaron, my brother, and his sons, Nadab, Abihu, Ithamar, and Eleazar went first. We were Levites. Priests. The leading family—with Moses talking to God all the time, and Aaron and his sons for priests. I would have played the timbrel. Beat the timbrel. But my timbrel was packed in the bundles with the kneading troughs. I walked through the sea as if dancing. I walked between the high walls of water on either side as if they were ordinary hills. "The water is singing to us," I said. "Keep going. Walk. Walk," I tell you. Walking through the water was like playing the timbrel. I heard the same sound.

Seven Days in Leprosy Camp

The Egyptians rode into the sea behind us. I heard the screams. We rushed—we hurried with fear. When all of us were across, Moses stretched out his hand over the sea, and it closed on Pharaoh's army.

I unpacked my timbrel, and the other women unpacked theirs, and we danced on the other side of the Red Sea. My voice rose about others. "Sing, sing," I said. "The Lord is my strength and salvation. The Lord is a man of war. Pharaoh's chariots he cast into the sea. His chosen captains drowned in the Red Sea. They sank to the bottom as a stone. With the blast of his nostrils, the waters were gathered. The floods stood upright as a heap, and the depths were congealed in the heart of the sea. The enemy said, 'I will pursue, I will overtake,' but you blew with your wind; the sea covered them, they sank to the bottom as lead. Who is like you, O Lord?" I took my timbrel and led the women in song and dance. The people shouted with a loud voice, "We will serve the Lord forever!"

All this I remembered in the leprosy tent. And yet the memories were not through.

We went into the wilderness of Shur, and there was nothing to drink. Six hundred thousand men, their wives and children, their flocks and herds were thirsty. We came to Marah, but could not drink the bitter waters. The people who had said, "We will serve the Lord forever," began to murmur. I could not rouse them. Moses cried to the Lord, "What will we drink?" The Lord showed Moses a tree. He cast it into the water, and we could drink.

At Elim, there were twelve wells and sufficient palm trees that cast their shade like the sound of a timbrel.

The manna came to us in the wilderness of Sin between Elim and Sinai. After 430 years of slavery, we had left Egypt, and now there was nothing to eat? The Hebrews murmured again: "In Egypt we had bread. What will we eat here? We should have died in Egypt, rather than in the wilderness with hunger."

Once again Moses prayed to the Lord, and said to the people, "The Lord has heard your murmurings and will provide food."

Why weren't they all covered with leprosy? What did I do that was worse?

It was like coriander seed, white, and tasted like wafers made with honey. The name of it was "manna," but what was it? It looked like hoarfrost on the ground.

We were riding high. Water came from the rock. When we wanted meat, quail fell from the sky.

Uprising of Goats

In the wilderness, manna fell like hoarfrost. No, it fell like leprosy. It flew like lice. It covered the ground like locust. It stunk like frogs if it was kept.

Moses kept writing. Writing and writing. Histories—record-keeping. *Write this for a memorial in a book. Write that,* the Lord God kept saying to Moses. Each day something happened. We walked. We set up camp. We dismantled camp. We walked. We walked. Would this walking never end?

Did Moses write, "Miriam has leprosy"? I would ask him to strike it from the book.

Why didn't God say, "Moses writes too much?"

History circles like a dream. It returns to something that needs attention—that needs to be provoked. A dream is a dance of return. Interpret if you can. A dancer danced to the edge of her dream and returned a dancer from the sea.

A priest of the Midianites named Jethro came to Moses with a woman and two boys. The woman was his daughter. The boys were Moses' sons, Gershom and Eliezer. My nephews. The woman was Moses' wife. Her name was Zipporah. A shepherdess from the desert where he fled from Egypt after he committed murder. This, his wife? This is what he was doing there?

"You sit here with the people before you night and day," Jethro said to Moses. "You'll wear down. Teach them your laws and appoint men of truth over them to be rulers of thousands, and rulers of hundreds, and rulers of fifties, and rulers of tens. Let them judge the people and bring to you the large matters. Then you will be able to endure."

Jethro went back to Midian without Zipporah. The dark wife of Moses sat with us, as if she belonged with us.

Did I not sing after the crossing? Did I not tell Pharaoh's daughter I would find a nurse for him? Did I not lead the women in dance? Did I not please the Lord?

I divided my memories among the spots of leprosy.

From Rephedim we traveled to Sinai, where Moses gathered the people before the mountain. We heard the thunderings and saw the lightning. A trumpet sounded. The people trembled. Where did the sound come from?

Moses went up into the mountain—into a thick cloud—and came back with the Commandments. Don't do this. Don't do that. I didn't like them. I didn't like her. How could I hold back?

"All you have said, we will do," the people answered.

There were days and days of writing. All the laws. The covenants. The ordinances. The judgments. All the orders from God. The offerings. The order of hosts. Rules. Rules.

"All you said, we will do."

I should have known how it would be . . .

Moses went up a second time to the mountain. This time he did not come back. Maybe an animal killed him. Maybe he was lost. The people said we needed a leader—it seemed right. Our ability to do what we wanted spread over us like a plague. We were afraid of our freedom with no one but the invisible God telling us the way. We had to have something we could see. We made a calf with the gold we brought out of Egypt. We had been with straw and brick so long, why wouldn't we want gold? Aaron helped the people make the calf. Did he not tell Moses, "I threw some gold in the fire, and the calf came out?" Did he receive leprosy for that?

No, we were all giddy again. We were reckless without Egyptian slave masters over us. We had gold. We had stripped the Egyptians. Despoiled them. After their first-born sons died, they wanted to get rid of us. "Here, take this, take that." My arms were heavy with gold bracelets. My ears heavy with gold earrings. We had crossed through a sea. We had seen the impossible.

But Moses was gone too long in the mountain. This time he was not coming back. We were without leadership. I took the earrings from my ears. I sang a song to the golden calf.

What happened to Moses? We wanted to move on! We were going to Canaan, to the land of our patriarchs. There were times we were clouded with our own misunderstanding. Not words—you could put your hand through them. We wanted something solid. There were Egyptians with us. They were the ones who said we had to be led by something *gleaming*.

Moses came down from the mountain and found us in disarray. He carried two stone tablets. He threw them at us.

"Who is with the Lord, come to me—Blot out their sins from your book," Moses roared. The Lord brought a plague on the people who did not repent. Several thousand died and were buried in the wilderness.

There were terrible times in the wilderness. It wasn't all dancing and merriment.

I helped Aaron because I wanted music.

Uprising of Goats

A stiff-necked people. Rebellious—wasn't that the meaning of my name?

On the journey, the Lord God was angry a lot. On the journey, we walked a lot. On the journey, Moses wrote a lot.

He described the tabernacle we were to build from the Lord's instructions. Its furniture. The brazen altar where we sacrificed animals. The laver. The lampstand. The table of bread. The altar of incense. The ark of the covenant. The linen curtains. The curtains woven from goat hair. And the order of the tribes around the tabernacle—four encamped on each side.

As I worked, I longed for music the way the Hebrews longed for quail. As I wove the goat hair for the tabernacle curtain, it felt like music in my hands. I could weave if I thought of it as music. Yes, I could sing—I have been necessary as a goat.

What did it matter—the great crossing the sea—if it all fell in around me afterwards?

We went into the wilderness as a mixed multitude. They were the ones who cried and complained, and caused their complaints to spill over into our people. And when the people complained, the Lord heard. His anger consumed the people with fire until Moses prayed to the Lord and the fire was quenched.

It was always Moses. The Lord's favorite. I felt the sores of bitterness inside me on this bitter journey of memory.

Manna continued to fall from heaven with the dew of evening. Still, we grumbled, "Who will give us more flesh to eat? How long had it been since we had quail?" The Egyptians who came with us remembered the fish they ate in Egypt, the cucumbers, melons, leeks, onions, and garlic of Egypt. They wanted something besides this manna. We gathered it. We ground it in mills, beat it in a mortar, baked it in pans, made cakes of it, and still it tasted like oil.

If we could we eat music, I would play for us.

The Lord spoke to Moses about more division of responsibilities. So Moses gathered seventy men, and they stood around the tabernacle until the Lord came down in a cloud and took the Spirit that was on Moses and gave it to the seventy men. When the Spirit rested upon them, they prophesied and did not stop. My mouth was open also, singing, praising. We remembered the crossing of the Red Sea. The patriarchs: Abraham, Isaac,

Seven Days in Leprosy Camp

Jacob, Joseph. We spoke of our journey to Canaan, back to the land of our forefathers. We spoke of battles ahead. We spoke fortitude into the people, strengthening them with the words of prophecy. We spoke of the Lord, our provider.

But that was before I ate leprosy.

Leprosy did not have sound. It was without a trimbrel. Without dance.

I was like hoarfrost. My skin was rippled with leprosy. When I combed my long hair, I saw it was white. I was the manna I had mocked. I had leprosy of the voice. I could not sing.

Isolation was more punishment than leprosy.

No, there was no pain. I could not feel my hands or feet. I was cut off from myself. It was not hard to stay in the tent. But what were the restless ones doing? The ones who wanted to stir? Move on? These were our years of release from Egypt. Our years of wandering to find our way to Canaan.

We perched on the little wagons in which we rode. We, the little she-goats.

When I sat in leprosy camp, I thought Moses continued his work of writing down laws and instructions. If an ox was accustomed to push with his horn, and his owner had not kept him in—if the ox gored—if the ox hurt someone—if I, Miriam, spoke against—if I spoke and spoke—then I would sit outside the camp. If I did not like black, then I could be white. Leprosy was God's writing on me. It was my book of humiliation.

I drank this bitterness in leprosy camp. I bent forward to bury my face. Had *I* murdered anyone? There it was—my rebellion—my little act of discontent. My *mealiness*. My pride. I came to a place in myself hard as a quail bone. I lay prostrate before the Lord. *I have murdered your presence before me.* I was there where little snakes coiled. I washed my face in them. *Forgive me.* I broke before God. *You are God. I am not. No, I should not have spoken against Moses' wife. I should not have resented the prophecies of others. I should not have given my earrings for a golden calf.* I was ashamed because of what I'd done before the Lord. His words stung like bees. Not the Lord God's, but Moses' words asking the Lord's mercy for me. Why wasn't Moses angry? Why didn't he say, "You should not speak against my wife?" Why was he so meek, he who was raised in the house of Pharaoh? He who had servants and owned the world?

I thought how seven days were a circle back to myself as I was, but with a new self with it. Washed in repentance. Or if not washed in repentance,

Uprising of Goats

I was washed in recognition of my shortcomings—my disobediences. I remembered Aaron's words to Moses, "My Lord, don't lay this sin upon us. We have done foolishly. We have sinned. Don't let her be as one dead, whose flesh is half consumed when she comes forth from her mother's womb." In the leprosy tent, outside the camp, I saw this consumption of flesh on my hands. Were they not once covered with pitch and slime for an ark of bulrushes?

A Chapter in Which There Is an Afterword to Miriam

They are walking in their sleep and try to wake themselves up with nightmares.
—G. K. Chesterton, *The Everlasting Man*

I brought you up out of the land of Egypt, and redeemed you out of the house of servants; and I sent before you Moses, Aaron, and Miriam.
—Mic 6:4

There were nights I dreamed of Miriam in the wilderness as Israel wandered for forty years between the Red Sea and the crossing of the Jordan River into Canaan. There were nights when their wanderings were clear as the sky.

I had been released from teaching for the summer. And though I had returned—though I was back in captivity—I still felt the wildness of release.

Israel had walked out of bondage in Egypt after four hundred years. I had walked out of teaching for three months. Now I was back to face the coursework that others faced with ease while I struggled with the brick and mortar of teaching. No wonder Miriam took issue with Moses.

Often I dreamed of upheaval in the night. The goats were uprising because the enemy was near. They knew a leopard was in the tall grass by the black river. They natted because of the danger of the world. Danger

Uprising of Goats

in extinction if their voices were not heard. I had trouble with leopards and leprosy. Something black as tar. All of it scrambled in my dreams. My dreams were filled with leprosy. Sleep was a leprosy tent.

Maybe the leopard would lie down with the hornets. No—it was the goats.

Had I passed through a wormhole back into another time? A warp in the cloth of time and space? The strings held us all together as long as they kept vibrating. But now I read an article on the flaws of string theory in a scientific journal. Physicists were still in search of a simple unifying theory. The theory of everything.

I think it was vibrating histories that I traveled, placing a sense of place, of space, upon the voices. Was it what I entered as I wrote?

Miriam, ca. 1430 bc.

> These are the journeys of the children of Israel, who went from the land of Egypt with their armies under the hand of Moses and Aaron. And Moses wrote their goings according to their journeys by the commandment of the Lord. On the next day, after the Passover, the children of Israel went out with a high hand in the sight of the Egyptians, for the Egyptians buried their first born which the Lord had smitten among them. And the children of Israel departed from Rameses and encamped in Succoth. And they departed from Succoth and encamped in Etham. They removed from Etham and turned again into Pihahiroth which is before Baalzephon and encamped before Migdol. They departed from Pihahiroth and passed through the midst of the sea into the wilderness. From there—Marah—Elim of the wells and palm trees—the wilderness of Sin—Dophkah—Alush—Rephidim, where there was no water—Sinai—Kibrothhattaavah—Hazelroth—Rithmah—Rimmonperez—Libnah—Rissah—Kehelathat—Mount Shepher—Haradah—Makheloth—Tahath—Terah—Mithkah—Hashmonah—Moseroth—Benejaakan—Horhagidgad—Jotbathah—Abronah—Eziongeber—Kadesh, in the wilderness of Zin, where Miriam died.
>
> —Num 33:1–36

What was I doing here? My worn briefcase full of student papers. The monotony of grading, though once in a while, one paper would lift above the others and I would be lost in reading.

A Chapter in Which There Is an Afterword to Miriam

There were faculty who always were gone. There were others who never left. Who knows what worlds of research and buried thoughts were behind the closed doors. At one time, there had been an open-door policy. At one time, there had been mandatory chapel. At one time, there had been a God.

UPRISING

A Chapter in Which the End Is Reached

Why was the Bible my field?

Because the hornets were swarming and had no place to go.

They were looking for a hive, which the Bible is.

I DON'T KNOW WHEN the voices stopped—or why they began to grow dimmer. They were silent for days, then I would hear something, but could make nothing of it. What visitations had come to me in the noise of the burdened world? The voices left their last delivery parallel to my life. Often when I wrote, I felt they were with me. Now they had gone back to their own places, wherever they were. Who knew why they had come or why they had left? I felt abandoned. It was like Pharaoh's dream of seven fat cows and seven lean. The rain had stopped. The burning heat replaced it, and I felt the drought and famine of voices. I had to return to my ordinary life without their *otherness*. It was one more parting. I swallowed a hard bone. This rock in the way. This wall I was broken against.

At first I missed them terribly. Then I grew used to my own voice in class. I grew used to students' papers spread out before me on the bed. I read their words, and afterwards thought about grading. Sometimes my daughters were in the house and I listened to their voices. Or I had e-mails or calls to answer with their concerns about boyfriends or their careers after college.

What had it been like before the voices?

I decided they were always there. But somehow I had heard them and had taken them with me for a while. Or maybe I followed them. Then their trail was lost. They went back to their own land, wherever it was they lived. But they had left their words on the page. I could almost hear them speaking there.

I was riled when I knew the book was finished. I was angry that I would have to get along without the voices. I felt they cut off too short. Maybe other voices would come later, but I felt an end to the current project.

I felt the combativeness of women. What secret war waged within. The leopard was the dementia that bothered my former mother-in-law. I also wanted to go to war, though I was supposed to want peace. My leopard was this reclusiveness. This desire to write what would irritate.

I made statements before I thought how they would go over with my colleagues. I said what I was thinking before I thought.

"Hitler did us a favor," I said at a department party. "Through him, we saw the pit of the human heart. We saw the regime, the state, the human heart on its own—when it has full power to do so."

Others had a horrified look on their faces. I tried to make light of it. Justine Crowd would make the most of it as time went on.

"Did you think this fabrication of voices would work?" a colleague asked later. "Did you want to look ridiculous in your zealotry?"

There was a word he had not used before. Was that what I was?

I read from the Scriptures in church one Sunday morning—the minister often asked a member of his congregation to read:

> I have blotted out, like a thick cloud, your transgressions, and, like a cloud, your sins; return to me; for I have redeemed you. Sing, O heavens; for the Lord has done it; shout, you lower parts of the earth; break forth into singing, you mountains, O forest, and every tree therein ... I am the Lord who makes all things; who stretches forth the heavens alone; who spreads abroad the earth by myself; who frustrated the token of the liars, and make diviners mad; who turns wise men backward, and makes their knowledge foolish.

—Isa 44:22–25

Was that a blessing? To me, it felt like a curse. I left the podium and sat down. The passage continued, but that was enough reading. The pastor looked at me, but I looked past him as if I had read to the end of the passage he had marked.

Now, just think about that for a while. Scripture was my staff. My encourager. My need.

As I sat in the pew, I thought for a moment I heard a noise like a small flock of goats on a distant hill. Maybe it was the organist with her hand on the stopper. It helped me remember that I went away as a woman. I came back as a goat. We are goats. All of us: goats.

I continued from time to time to hear the goats when the organ squeaked, or when the chapel bell on campus chimed, or when the church bell pealed in my neighborhood, or when the birds stammered at the feeder.

I felt I was there when the women stood together in heaven, though apparently there's no gender in heaven. They knew who they were—from different ages, places, circumstances. I looked at their voices on the pages I had written. I held them a few more years.

I continued to think of the Scriptures during the sermon. All of it had been written on goatskin. Or stalks of papyrus, stripped, dried, and flattened. It took eight goats to write a book like Romans. It could be called the uprising of Scripture because it was ignored, or looked at as history, or a text for study in comparative religions. It took time to understand. Somehow, I recognized the voices calling. The ordinary, unrecognized voices here on this mysterious mountainside in the pasture recognized as life.

Acknowledgments

THE JEROME AND THE General Mills Foundation in Minnesota for a travel and research grant to Caesarea and Hierapolis. Gratefulness to Sue Ellen Dobb, my guide, and Ali Taylan, my driver in Turkey. Gratefulness to Michael Nelson, my guide and driver in Israel.

Acknowledgment to the Visiting Writer Fellowship at the Institute of Faith and Learning, Baylor University, Waco, Texas, where much of the writing of the first draft of "The Parting" was done.

Gratefulness to Macalester College for a sabbatical during that time.

Acknowledgment also to the "Introduction to New Testament Literature" course and Professor Mikeal C. Parsons, Baylor University.

Acknowledgment to a first reading of the manuscript at the Spring 2003 Art and Soul: Mystery and Meaning Conference of Religion and the Arts, Baylor University, Waco, Texas, March 20–22, 2003.

Acknowledgment to a further reading during the Woods Lectures, Dubuque Theological Seminary, Dubuque, Iowa, April 21–22, 2003, and to Ann Hoch, who loaned me her videotape of Caesarea and a helpful book by Page, Charles R. II, and Carl Volz, *The Land and the Book: An Introduction to the World of the Bible* (Nashville: Abingdon, 1993).

I also thank my Chrysostom friends for listening.

Thankfulness also to Bethel Christian Fellowship in Saint Paul, Minnesota.

Gratefulness also to Azusa Pacific University.

An earlier version of "Dorcas: The Closets of Heaven: A chapter in which fabric is a weighty matter" was published as Glancy, Diane, *The Closets of Heaven* (Tucson, AZ: Chax, 1999).

Uprising of Goats

An earlier version of "Michal: A Stone I Could Not Lift: A Chapter Found on the Slope of a Steep Hill" was previously published as Glancy, Diane, "A Stone I Could Not Lift," *Ruminate Magazine* 13 (2009) http://www.ruminatemagazine.com/issue-13-confession/.

An earlier version of "Anna, A Chapter in Which a Raisin Cake Is Wrapped in Cloth" was previously published as Glancy, Diane, "A Raisin Cake Wrapped in Cloth: Anna, a Prophetess," *Books & Culture* 18 (2012) http://www.ctlibrary.com/bc/2012/novdec/raisin-cake-wrapped.html.

www.ingramcontent.com/pod-product-compliance
Lightning Source LLC
Chambersburg PA
CBHW050816160426
43192CB00010B/1779